# The Matthew Hayden Cookbook

## STORIES AND RECIPES FROM AUSTRALIA'S GOURMET CRICKETER

ABC
Books

Foreword by Justin Langer    5
Foreword by Luke Mangan    6
Introduction    8

## Seafood

Matty's mussels    10
Crumbed snapper    14
Calypso crayfish    18
Chilli Mumbai lagoon crabs    22
Salt-crusted red emperor    26
Fish pie    30
Steamed coral trout Thai style    34
Prawn and scallop skewers    38
Roy's calamari    42
Seafood gumbo    46

# Contents

## Chicken

Nola's chicken pie    50
Crispy chicken    54
Kell's asparagus chicken casserole    58
Chicken curry    62
Macadamia and feta stuffed chicken    66

## Meat

Smoked ham and pumpkin soup    70
Grandma's shepherd's pie    74
South African braai (BBQ)    78
Bangers and mash    82
Gabby's lasagne    86
Traditional spaghetti sauce    90
Roast lamb shanks    94
Straddie pizza    98

## Salads, Sides and Stuff

Mango chutney    102
Dhal    106
Bruschetta    110
Camembert dream pie    114
Cheese risotto    118
Cucumber salad    122
Avocado and mango salad    126

## Desserts

Vanilla slice    130
Coffee cheesecake    134
Mum's chocolate and macadamia nut pudding    138
Honey-iced coffee cake    142
Simple pavlova    146

Acknowledgments    150

# Foreword by Justin Langer

The obvious link between Matty Hayden and me is cricket. For over a decade we've followed similar career paths for our respective States, and more recently with the Australian cricket team. In the last few years we have had the opportunity to forge a very enjoyable and hopefully fruitful opening partnership within the Australian Test team.

The public knows us best for our on-field relationship, but we have enjoyed just as many good times off the field as we have with our baggy green caps sitting proudly on our heads.

One of the lines in Cold Chisel's song 'Flame Trees' goes 'I'm happy just to sit here round a table with old friends and see which one of us can tell the biggest lies'. Every time I hear these words, I think of Haydos and me sitting around with our mates or wives, listening to good music, laughing, 'talking rubbish and telling lies', and invariably drinking good wine or coffee and eating even better food.

If there is one thing we both love besides our families, our friends and our country, it is our food! Over the years I have been fortunate enough to have tested many of Matt's recipes. Special feasts have included such delights as seafood banquets, marinated, roasted and barbecued meats, pastas to die for and risottos that make your mouth water.

At my place, two nights before he scored his 380 at the Waca, Matt decided he would act as chef for the night. As if my kitchen were his own, he went about his business with the same care and concentration as he did with the bat in his hand two days later. Red emperor roasted in coconut milk and Thai herbs and chillies was served up with a seafood paella that any of the most renowned Spanish chefs would have been proud to call their own. Like his record-breaking innings, our dinner was quite simply magnificent.

Haydos culinary treats have been as consistent as his runs. I have never known someone to enjoy their cooking as much as my big mate. He is meticulous in his preparation and creative in his ideas. He has been interested in acquiring recipes and information from all over the globe and he has not been backward in giving it a go in kitchens in the most remote parts of the world. As a result, he backs himself to serve up a spread fit for kings. And it is as kings that we have so often eaten, thanks to the king himself.

It has been said that a great life is nothing more than a series of great memories woven together. For me, great memories usually involve wonderful company, excellent music, lots of laughter and fantastic food.

I have no doubt that this book can play a major part in your next great memory. It will certainly inspire me to get my hands dirty in the kitchen and I hope it inspires you to enjoy one of life's greatest pleasures.

Have fun with this book, you will not be disappointed.

# Foreword by Luke Mangan

We all know that Matthew Hayden is one of the greatest cricketers in the world, and it takes great determination and hard work to get to the top in any field.

But what some of you probably didn't know is that Matthew has a great passion for food. As part of his world travels he's become something of a gourmand, from blue cheese and honey mussels in Cannes and spiced crayfish in the Caribbean to chill crabs in Mumbai and mango chutney in Sri Lanka.

Haydos, as his friends like to call him, has eaten in places I've only dreamed about and this book is a delicious collection of his travels and experiences, culinary and otherwise.

While the colourful stories about exotic places and people in this book attest to his worldly adventures, the recipes attest to his skill as a great home cook. Or so I've been told. I'm still waiting for that dinner party invite, Haydos! (That's the problem with being a chef, no one ever invites you over for a meal!)

Anyway, back to the book. I met Matthew several years ago when he and his lovely wife Kellie first started coming to my Sydney restaurant Salt. They're now regulars but I also count them as friends.

Matthew's not only one of the friendliest and most down-to-earth people you'll ever meet, but also his generosity is unsurpassed. It's through his work with charities that we became friends and the Salt team continue to cook for Haydos at charity events whenever the occasion calls for it.

So, while Matthew's record as a formidable cricket player has been well-documented, now his culinary talent is on record as well. This book is a great achievement, the recipes are full of flavour and simple to cook.

# Introduction

Ever since I can remember, food has been important to me. My dad summed it up early on when he claimed I was born with a knife and fork in my hands! I remember I seemed to be hungry all the time, probably because I was such an active kid, with cricket practice or the flavour-of-the-month activity filling my afternoons after school. I never really started to think seriously about cricket until I was in my second year at university, partly because I never had the build of your typical opening batsmen. I was huge even as a youngster: genetics aside, I was a little too partial to tucking into too much food!

Many memorable moments in my life involve food. Like most people, I enjoy eating good food, but I love cooking just as much. Part of the reason for this was my grandmother, Katherine Mary Hayden. Grandma was a simple woman with strong family values and traditions. She meant the world to me. I'd sit for hours talking to Grandma about her childhood. Watching her at work in her small kitchen, I was fascinated by how she could combine a few simple ingredients to produce amazing flavors. Looking back, I probably annoyed the heck out of her with my incessant questions, but her responses were beautiful, perfect poetry to my young, impressionable ears, 'It's simple, darling, it is just a pinch of salt and a cup of flour along with a whole lot of love!'

Grandma was a special woman who made me feel like I was the most loved person on earth. When she passed away in the mid 1990s, part of me died as well. Fortunately, her memories live on in the Hayden household through the recipes she handed down with her blessings. They reflect the simple pleasures that are often missing in our busy, modern lives. Little gifts of love made with precision, things like jam drops, Anzac cookies, rice puddings, homemade jams, chutneys and preserves. Grandma taught me the value of taking the time to enjoy my family by experiencing together one of life's simple pleasures: food!

Food is a powerful reminder of the various roads I have travelled. Whether it's downtown New York or the James Street Markets in Brisbane, food reflects a city's culture and its people's way of life. Wherever I go, I love to sit people-watching, to see life unfolding in front of my eyes. My career as a professional athlete has given me so much opportunity to fulfil this passion. It has opened doors to so many interesting food experiences and I've delighted in meeting a whole range of people and culinary experts from different cultures, including the chefs from some of the world's leading restaurants and hotels.

Food is the fuel which has enabled me to reach my potential as an athlete. Becoming knowledgeable about my diet and modifying various recipes to suit my needs has allowed me to recover from training and competitions more rapidly, to keep my weight in check and, most importantly, to remain healthy and happy. To achieve at the elite level of anything in life requires dedication and determination. And being competitive

means you are always looking for that edge to keep you ahead of the pack.  My philosophy is simple: eat fresh food from all the five food groups every day.

A family that eats together stays together, I reckon. It makes me so proud to see my little girl Grace enjoying eating great food that my wife Kellie and I have cooked for her. Our meals together are up there with the best times I've ever had. I hope you enjoy the recipes in my book with your own families, too.

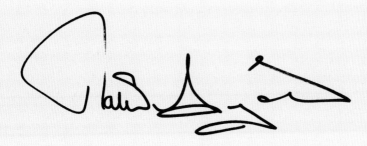

# Matty's mussels

Kellie and I were enjoying the beautiful sun-drenched south of France when we came across the most succulent mussels dish we have ever tasted.

There is much travel involved during an English county season and there's only a small window of opportunity of, say, four days to break away from cricket commitments and get away from it all. With the charm of Europe so close, a lightning trip over the English Channel is a temptation too good to refuse.

Leaving tiresome travel between matches behind, we took a break from the rigours of county cricket in England, flew to Monaco, hired a car and drove to Cannes.

During the flight, Kellie was seated in business class and I was down the back in 'cattle class'. On arrival at Monaco airport she said to me, 'You wouldn't believe who was on our flight – Richie Benaud!'

'No way!' I said. 'Come on, Kell. You've got to be kidding! I reckon you've got him confused with someone else.'

But Kell was adamant. 'No! No!' she said. 'It was Richie.'

Anyway, I rocked up to the baggage collection and – blow me down! – there was Richie in his beige suit. 'Well, fancy seeing you here!' he said to me.

'Yeah! I thought the same actually, Richie. Kell told me you were here but I didn't believe her. So, what're you up to?'

Richie answered in his trademark manner, heavily stressing the final consonants of words. 'Just thought I'd take a little break. Daphne and I own a little unit in the south of France. Not, ah, really very big. Not big ... at all really! Just, ah, big enough to swing a cat. And,' he added with a glint in his eye, 'to swing Daphne now and then! Really marvellous stuff! Really!'

It's always good to catch up with Richie. He's a top bloke and he and his wife really enjoy their breaks when they get a pause in Richie's English television commentary commitments on the BBC.

So we parted company with Richie, hired the car, and off we went.

A glorious atmosphere envelops you in Cannes. High on a hill, there is a cathedral that dominates the horizon. Narrow cobblestone streets wind, snake-like, up the hill for a kilometre. With each step you take, you feel like you're stepping on history. It's like an aura that permeates the whole place. An amazing city!

On the way up we came across this little restaurant that specialises in mussels. They serve blue cheese and honey-mustard mussels in a

large pot, with a fresh French stick that you use for dipping into the cheese and mustard sauce. It is so simple and beautifully presented, and so easy to eat. There we were, eating mussels, sipping on a little French bubbly, under sun-drenched skies while the sea lapped at the shore. It was awesome!

So that is where my taste for mussels comes from.

At North Straddie, there is a local bloke, Mal Paskin, who is one of the few remaining fishmongers on the island. Whenever we're there, we stop by to pick up a couple of bags of his green-lipped mussels, throw them in the pot with some wine, tomatoes and herbs, and tuck in.

1 kg green-lipped mussels

1 tablespoon butter

1 onion, finely chopped

4 garlic cloves, crushed

1 red chilli, finely chopped

2 ripe tomatoes, chopped (about 300 g)

400 g can diced tomatoes

2 cups (500 ml) white wine (chardonnay
    or sauvignon blanc)

½ teaspoon chilli powder

salt and pepper, to taste

small handful of fresh coriander, chopped

1 tablespoon extra virgin olive oil

# Matty's mussels

Have some hot crusty bread on the side for mopping up the delicious sauce – you won't want to waste a drop.

Scrub the mussels and pull off the beards.

Heat the butter in a very large pot and add the onion, garlic, fresh chilli and fresh tomatoes. Cook over a medium heat until soft.

Add the canned tomatoes, half the white wine and the chilli powder. Bring to the boil, then reduce the heat and simmer the sauce for 20 minutes. Season with salt and pepper.

Add the remaining white wine and the mussels to the pot. Bring back to the boil and cover with a tightly fitting lid. Steam for 10 minutes, until all the mussels have opened (discard any that don't open after this time).

Serve sprinkled with coriander and drizzled with olive oil.

SERVES 4

# Crumbed snapper

One of the great things about life on Queensland's North Stradbroke Island is the people I meet. Take, for example, Andrew Mirosch, a renowned chef who now resides with his beautiful young family on Straddie. He is a champion bloke; a real character, too, with dreadlocks in his hair and built like an outhouse!

Andrew is such an uncomplicated person and I guess that's the reason we get on so well, even though we come from such different professions. When we are together he doesn't want to talk about cooking and I don't want to talk about cricket. But we share a love of fishing, much to our partners' frustrations. There have been times when we have 'conned' our lovely ladies into allowing us a day out on the boat – pushing all the limits of household harmony, we head out as early as we can and arrive home as late as we can!

On one occasion we planned to fish an area known as 'The Cathedrals' just outside Moreton Bay, but had to wait for the weather to break. This turned into a game of patience, but the wait was worth it: when Andrew and I got out there, we cleaned up! Andrew reckons I ate 3½ kilos of snapper by myself that day, which is probably on the money.

Snapper come from deep waters to breed in the shallow waters of North Straddie during June, July and August. Fishing for snapper is just the ultimate break!

With fishing, you have to be so dedicated – and I'm passionate about my fishing! I have a saying: 'If you miss the finer details, then you never unlock the key to a fishing spot.' By this I mean that if you don't put in the time, effort

and preparation, you mostly come home disappointed. It is a big ocean; and while you have to have luck, people who have the knowledge generally catch the fish.

We caught six or seven really good eating snapper, much to the delight of my daughter, Grace, who was 15 months old at the time. One of these fish was only a couple of inches bigger than she was, and she danced around it saying, 'Ish! Ish!'

Our celebration of the fishing day came through as a magnificent meal of Crumbed snapper that night.

# Crumbed snapper

4 snapper fillets, skin removed
½ cup (60 g) cornflour
salt and pepper
4 eggs
1½ cups (150 g) breadcrumbs
1 cup (250 ml) extra virgin olive oil
1 garlic clove, halved
sprig of rosemary
⅓ cup (80 ml) lemon juice
⅓ cup (80 ml) balsamic vinegar

This is a perfect meal for the start of summer, served with a simple green salad with a zesty dressing.

Put the cornflour onto a plate and season with salt and pepper. Lightly beat the eggs in a shallow bowl, and put the breadcrumbs onto another plate. Dust the snapper fillets in cornflour, dip into the egg, then coat with breadcrumbs. Set aside on a plate.

Heat the oil, garlic and rosemary in a heavy-based frying pan until very hot. Cook the snapper fillets in two batches for about 2 minutes each side, until golden brown. Transfer to a plate lined with paper towels.

Drain out the oil and wipe the crumbs out of the pan with a paper towel. Return the garlic and rosemary to the pan. Add the balsamic vinegar and simmer for about 4 minutes, until reduced by a third. Add the lemon juice and season with salt and pepper to taste.

Serve the fish with the sauce on the side for drizzling.

SERVES 4

# Calypso crayfish

There is a bar on the West Indian island of Antigua called Lashings. It sits on a beach – just about anywhere you go in the West Indies is on a beach. And if you're not on the beach, then you're in the water, because that is what the West Indies is – a place of white sandy beaches and crystal-clear blue water. The bar has a wooden floor that sits half a metre above the sand. It is more or less a grass hut! I have always thought that if a strong northerly wind blew, there wouldn't be much of Lashings left.

Lashings is owned by Curtly Ambrose and Richie Richardson – two of the West Indies' finest ever cricketers. Ambrose and Richardson lured Australian cricketers for years like a snake charmer lures snakes, talking themselves up and telling Australians how good they were – and they were!

I can vividly recall the times when Curtly would amble out to a Test wicket and address only the captain. A man of a few words, he would acknowledge him with a simple 'Skipper!'.

But put a cricket ball in his hand and his focus would be only on the batsman. And as an Australian opening batsman, I can tell you it was not a pretty sight: his huge frame, relaxed and focused totally on me from the opposite end of a cricket pitch, starting his run.

And then the West Indian antics would start. Firstly, there would be a clap of hands from somewhere and a voice would say, 'Ooooh! I tink we're in bus'ness here, mun!' As a team, they had a distinctive way of

repeating themselves, very quickly: 'Yea, mun! We in bus'ness here, mun!' That would start the ramble: 'I t'ink he wan' to hook, eh, mun!' This would be followed by laughter. Another would add, 'Get 'im on a stepladder, mun! On a stepladder!' Then, more advice: 'Waist an' chin, Amby! Waist an' chin!'

Then in would come the ball like a bullet. Crash! The 'death rattle'!

I have a very vivid memory of Curtly scattering my stumps during the Boxing Day Test. I can still see that blasted stump rolling over the deck from a ball that struck the wicket so hard it almost followed me back to the pavilion!

The West Indies thrives on music, and so, too, do the cricket spectators! There is always a carnival atmosphere at their grounds.

Calypso music, bongo drums, instruments of all kinds, colourful characters, and singing and dancing can be heard from all parts of the ground. In fact, every ground has huge speakers installed on the buildings. If the West Indian cricket team records a win, especially against the Australians, the whole stadium turns into something that resembles an American hip hop night club. It's party time – big time!

That same atmosphere extends to Lashings.

Every Friday and Saturday night, Curtly and Richie can be found at Lashings – Curtly on his guitar and Richie on his drums, jamming until the wee small hours of the morning. When we were touring in 2003, the West Indies won a Test and everybody was in celebration mode. The whole beach around Lashings was packed with people as Curtly and Richie jammed away.

That's the wild side of Lashings, but it has another personality as well. Wander down mid-week, or even midday on a weekend, and it is a tranquil place where water lapping peacefully on the sand replaces the beat of Richie's drums. It's as good as it gets, with water the colour of the sky, and rich green foliage swaying around the headland.

At Lashings, Kell, Grace and I joined Steve Waugh and his wife, Lynette, for lunch. For $US25 you get these massive crayfish. West Indians love their spices, so you'll often find coloured spices sprinkled over the crayfish and a wedge of green lime on the side. Imagine, against the backdrop of the beautiful blue of the ocean and white of the sand, these gloriously painted crayfish with red tinges and white flesh, dappled with colourful spices and lime. Such contrasting colours! Magic!

Afterwards, you slide down off your chair, onto the beach and into the water like a dirty big croc. You just bask in the Caribbean sunshine. You make an entire afternoon of lunch at Lashings.

SEAFOOD

# Calypso crayfish

4 whole, uncooked crayfish (rock lobster)
200 g butter
1 rasher bacon, finely chopped
1 onion, finely chopped
2 garlic cloves, crushed
1 lime, quartered
splash of Tabasco sauce
salt and pepper

Serve these with salad for the health conscious, or if the waistline is not an issue serve with hot chips and cold beer.

Chop the crays in half and clean in salty water.

Preheat a chargrill or BBQ plate until hot. Place the crayfish halves flesh side down onto the grill to sear the flesh.

Flip onto the shells for 8-10 minutes, until cooked through (the shell will turn pink and the flesh will be white).

Meanwhile, melt the butter in a frying pan and brown the bacon, onion and garlic.

Place the cooked crays onto a plate and spoon on the browned bacon and onion mixture.

Splash on Tabasco sauce and top that off with a squeeze of lime juice, to taste. Season with salt and pepper.

SERVES 4

# Chilli Mumbai lagoon crabs

I have special memories of India and Mumbai, and I may even be a bit biased towards the country, the people, the city and its cuisine because it was in India that I was able to launch my 'second' career with Australia. When we toured in 2001, the first Test of the series was in Mumbai. That was the Test when Gilly and I put on a tremendous partnership when a win looked doubtful. It was a Test we ended up winning – the only Test win of the tour!

It was so rewarding just because I was under so much pressure. To be frank, if I had not performed on that tour, I would not be playing for Australia today and I certainly would not be writing about the foods of the world.

The irony about batting in the pressure of a Test match in India is that the middle of the pitch is one of only two truly peaceful places in the country. The other is your hotel room.

In the middle of the cricket ground, you are protected from the masses by a barrier, so, aside from the eleven players trying to get you out, there is no one interfering with you. You are competing with the ball and that is all. Thus, it remains a very peaceful place.

That said, you can always hear the Indian crowd. They're always 'on fire'. The Indian crowds tend to have loud, highly pitched voices and play drums, whistles and horns. You can even smell the unique odours of Mumbai from food stalls.

The foods are quite colourful and they have chilli on everything. In India, they even have chilli on lollies. If the food does not have chilli on it, it is not an option.

I guess this is why, when you come home to Australia and have steak and chips, you miss the different flavours that enhance the food in places like India. The chilli and unique spices of the subcontinent are almost an addiction.

Your room is also a sanctuary from the teeming masses. You can just close your door to the world. But even in that room, there is a fine line. When you order room service, the waiter comes to the door along with another ten people! Everything is ten times busier. Look around you now – when you see a person, multiply that person by ten and you'll have an idea of what India is like.

Mumbai has roughly the same population as Australia in an area probably not as big as Brisbane. But it is part of the charm of the place, and your affection for Mumbai grows out of the chaos.

I was speaking with Indian batting ace Rahul Dravid last summer while the Indian team were in Australia. I asked him, 'Rahul, what do you reckon is the big difference between Australia and India?'

He answered quite simply, 'Oh, there is so much space!'

He went on to say he could walk around town shopping in Brisbane without being mobbed. 'In India, I have not been shopping for over a decade. I can't walk around India without being mobbed, let alone shop!'

Rahul Dravid is a national hero – in India, thousands of people wait to mob him wherever he goes. Believe it or not, he said he missed the attention while touring Australia.

Reminiscing, he turned to me and said, 'I miss the affection of the people, the way they make us feel like heroes. I miss the sights, the smells.'

There is no place like home. I can vouch for that and so, too, can Rahul Dravid.

SEAFOOD

4 uncooked crabs

1 tablespoon vegetable oil

2 red onions, halved and thinly sliced

6 curry leaves or 3 bay leaves

2 stalks lemon grass, white part only, finely sliced

3 slices ginger

4 garlic cloves, sliced

2 green chillies, seeds removed, finely chopped

2 tomatoes, peeled and chopped

2 teaspoons salt

1 teaspoon ground turmeric

2 tablespoons ground sweet paprika

1 tablespoon fragrant curry powder

1–2 teaspoons chilli powder

½ cup (125 ml) water

2 cups (500 ml) coconut milk

juice of 1 lime

# Chilli Mumbai lagoon crabs

This crab is best eaten with your hands, mixing the coconut curry sauce with steamed basmati rice. A magic meal!

Clean the crabs by lifting the small flap underneath and removing the shell. Pull off the gills underneath, and rinse away all the innards. Cut in half through the body, leaving the legs attached. Crush the claws slightly so the flavours can penetrate to the meat.

Heat the oil in a very large pot and fry the onions until soft and light brown. Add the curry leaves, lemon grass, ginger, garlic and green chillies. Fry for about 2 minutes, until fragrant.

Add the tomatoes, salt, turmeric, paprika and the curry and chilli powders. Stir well to combine.

Add the crabs and stir to coat in the mixture. Add the water and bring to boil. Reduce the heat to medium low, cover and cook for 10 minutes, then add the coconut milk. When it just comes to the boil again, simmer for another 10 minutes. Stir in the lime juice just before serving.

— *To peel tomatoes, score a little cross in the bottom and put into a heatproof bowl. Cover with boiling water and leave for a couple of minutes. Lift out, cool, then peel the skin off.*

SERVES 4

# Salt-crusted red emperor

Wherever I have travelled in the world, I have always taken my fly-fishing rod and fly-tier with me. And it was my fly-rod that, indirectly, led me to discovering the wonders of Salt-crusted red emperor.

In Galle, Sri Lanka, I stayed on the waterfront at a magic place called the Light House Hotel that, appropriately, beamed a light into the darkness to warn ships of the nearby coastline. In the morning I went for walks along the beach, watching the locals fish along the way. It was a fascinating sight! They stood with cane poles that had a string attached to the end, and they would pull out bait fish with no matter of fuss.

If you ever went to a school fête as a child, you may recall fishing with a stick that had a string attached and a fish-hook secured to its end. There would be a pool of water filled with little tin fish. The object of the game was to use your 'fishing line' to pull up a tin fish. If you hooked a fish, you won a prize.

Well, this is like everyday fishing in Sri Lanka. The people catch what they call mackerel, but it is really

bait fish. Watching them fish gave me the urge to produce my fly-rod and see what I could catch standing on some rocks next to the beach.

This was in 1999 and I had not played a Test in Sri Lanka at that stage. I was just a squad member, little known to the locals, I am sure. Within five minutes of my fishing, 100 people had encircled me. I thought to myself, 'Gee! I'm popular.' I had a great hour or so!

When I finally came down from the rocks, one of the Sri Lankans approached me and asked me to come back to his village. I thought what a friendly group of people they were and did not hesitate. But when I arrived at the village, I soon realised I was not the star attraction. My seven-weight fly-rod and my flashy flies were the centre of attention!

I bargained with one of the locals: 'Listen, mate, I'll teach you to throw a fly-rod if you teach me how to cook a fish in true Sri Lankan tradition.'

Now, by good fortune, the fellow with whom I had bargained just happened to be a chef at the hotel where we were staying. I couldn't believe my luck!

So, back at the hotel, he had the catch of the day ready to cook up. It was like a jewfish, similar to the ones you get in Western Australia, black in colour, not silver like the ones we have in Queensland. It was a magnificent fish! I told the Aussie boys to forget about the buffet that night – I was cooking them fish! 'Yeah! Sure you are!' was echoed in disbelief. So I took up residence in the kitchen and that chef taught me how to cook it.

He covered it in salt and placed it in the oven. The salt formed a hard crust on the outside, about 2 centimetres thick. When it was cooked, we poured brandy on it, lit it up like any top-class chef would do, and I carried it out to the waiting Australian cricket team on a big baking tray, smiling as I went.

Mind you, I had my fingers crossed. Being the tour rookie, I was desperate to save face! When the flame went out, I got my knife under the shell of salt and slowly moved it around the fish, lifting the salty crust off as I went. And then, *voila*! My beautiful steamed fish was revealed.

There were no complaints about the food that night! That evening the chef also showed me how to make a Sri Lankan seafood risotto.

Again, there was the reward for opening myself up to other people. I could have easily declined the invitation to the village and gone back into the protective cocoon of the hotel. But … look what I would have missed out on!

SEAFOOD

# Salt-crusted red emperor

2 kg red emperor, cleaned
12 egg whites
1 kg finely crushed sea salt
1 red chilli, finely chopped
1 teaspoon finely chopped fresh ginger
2 garlic cloves, finely chopped
1 lime, finely sliced
⅓ cup (80 ml) brandy, optional

Preheat the oven to 200°C.

Put the egg whites into a clean, dry bowl. Using electric beaters, beat until stiff peaks form. Fold in the sea salt to form a thick paste.

Spread half the salt mixture onto a large baking tray. Lay the fish on the salt mixture, and put the chilli, ginger, garlic and lime slices into the abdominal cavity.

Spread the remaining salt mixture over the fish to enclose completely; it should be 1–2 cm thick. Place into the oven and bake for 40 minutes.

To serve, cut around the mid line of crust and remove the top. It may crumble, but just pull off in large pieces.

If you like, pour brandy over the fish and immediately light to flambé. Serve straight from the baking tray.

SERVES 6

# Fish pie

Over in Western Australia, there is a mate of Justin 'Alfie' Langer's who supplies crayfish to the global market. Now it has become a tradition that during a Test match in the west, he comes in with a massive box of crayfish and prawns.

We sit around after a Test match, having a few glasses of wine, or some beers, and not only chew the fat, but also chew into these massive cooked crayfish, banana prawns and spotted prawns.

In October of 2003, on one of the last nights of the Test where I scored 380 against Zimbabwe, I was around at Alfie's house looking to break my run of the Hyatt Hotel's smoked ham and pumpkin soup that I had lived on as an evening meal. Alfie's mate loaded us up with all the seafood in the ocean. He brought around prawns, squid and scallops. All the boys were there – it was a feast for kings!

He also brought around this fish pie. Absolutely succulent! A beautiful meal! It had the boys lining up for seconds.

400 g fish fillets, cubed (red emperor is great)

200 g prawn meat

200 g scallop meat

200 g mussel meat

1 tablespoon olive oil

1 onion, finely diced

2 garlic cloves, crushed

1½ cups (375 ml) milk

2 teaspoons cornflour or arrowroot

1 teaspoon chopped fresh oregano

salt and pepper, to taste

50g butter, melted

3 sheets filo pastry

# Fish pie

Preheat the oven to 180°C.

Put all the seafood into a 6-cup capacity greased ovenproof dish. Heat the oil in a medium saucepan and cook the onion and garlic until soft and lightly golden. Add the milk to the pan and warm through. Put the cornflour into a small bowl and add a little of the milk. Stir to make a smooth paste, then add to the pan. Stir over low heat until thickened. Stir in the oregano, and season with salt and pepper.

Pour the sauce over the seafood and stir to combine. Brush the sheets of filo with melted butter, one at a time, and stack together. Fold in half and lay over the top of the pie mixture. Tuck or fold in the edges. Brush with butter.

Bake for 30 minutes, until crisp and golden, then serve immediately.

SERVES 4

# Steamed coral trout Thai style

When I am at Justin and Sue Langer's house in Perth, I feel like I'm in my own home. For one reason or another, Kell has never been to Western Australia with me, so the Langers have been my adoptive family in the west. I am usually looking for a bit of company and I couldn't think of a better way to spend some time than with Alfie, Sue and their beautiful family of three children. Alfie loves food as much as I do. Our stomachs are often the key to our conversation. In fact, more often than not, no matter where we are in the world, Alf will make a call to the tune of, 'Hey mate, how do you make those chilli mussels again?', in the enthusiastic manner only Alf has. However, during down-time from cricket in the West, I go to their place, rest, and then eat around the dinner table like I would at home.

I sometimes give Sue a list of things to gather from the shop and I will prepare a meal, either on their outstanding barbecue or in this great kitchen they have. I come around early afternoon, while Alfie and Sue go about their normal business, and prepare a meal.

Fortunately, Western Australia is blessed with an incredible supply of beautifully fresh fish, in particular red emperor. However, I don't think there is a better fish than coral trout, with its beautiful white flesh and firm texture. Throw in some chilli and garlic, olive oil, wrap it in foil, put it on the barbecue and simply steam it in its natural juices. So simple – just remember not to overcook it. Barbecues can be a little tricky in controlling heat and basically the only way that you can ruin a good piece of fish is to overcook it.

The Langers' house is a perfect spot and it's always a great occasion to be there. It's not too often you get to relax and enjoy someone cooking a meal for you in your own house, but I love doing it for the Langers.

2 teaspoons peanut or vegetable oil

1 onion, halved and finely sliced

2 spring onions, finely sliced (keep the white
and green separate)

3 garlic cloves, finely sliced

1 red bird's-eye chilli, seeds removed, finely sliced

1 kg whole coral trout, cleaned

400 g can low-fat coconut milk

4 cm piece ginger, cut into fine strips

handful of coriander leaves

# Steamed coral trout Thai style

Serve with a tomato and basil salad, and some steamed jasmine rice.

Preheat the oven to 180°C.

Heat the oil in a frying pan and cook the onion, the white part of the spring onions, garlic and chilli until soft. Stuff this mixture into the cavity of the fish.

Line a large baking dish with foil. Lay the fish onto the foil and lift the foil up around the fish. Pour the coconut milk over the fish, and sprinkle on the ginger. Cover with foil and fold the edges together to form a tight seal. Bake for 45 minutes, until the flesh flakes when tested with a fork.

To serve, carefully open the foil and scatter the coriander and green part of the spring onions over the fish.

SERVES 4

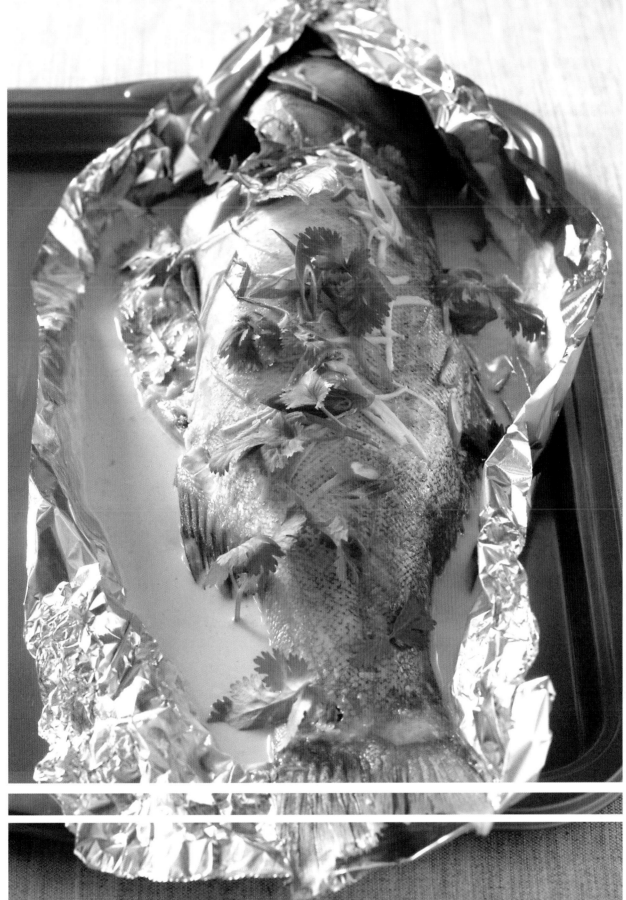

# Prawn and scallop skewers

How blessed with seafood we are in Australia and what a Mecca Darwin is for sports fishermen! It has fishing like you wouldn't believe, and a huge variety of fish. There is a perception that if you do not catch a barramundi in Northern Territory waters, then your trip is unsuccessful, but that's a statement I disagree with very strongly.

If you catch anything that moves really quickly, then you've had a victory in the NT waterways. I reckon it has the best fishing ever. And it is an adventure for every second of the day.

On a visit to Darwin during the Test series versus minnows, Bangladesh, I bumped into my long-time friend, Ben Dark, who, believe it or not, escaped from the big smoke to become a fishing local in Darwin.

'Mate, this place just gets into ya blood. You'd be hopeless, Haydos, up here. You'd never wear the baggy green again!' he said with a cheeky grin.

You look at the water and your imagination runs away with you. Your instincts take over, telling you what you could be catching and how you could be catching it. The waters are so bountiful!

A great bloke with a vast knowledge of the North is John Dumphey, who, though he lives in Sydney's Cronulla, has the best fishing contacts around. Why wouldn't he? He is, after all, the owner of Shimano Fishing Australasia and one of my great mates.

John knows a father and son, George and Ronny Voukolos, who run Fishing & Outdoor World tackle store in Darwin.

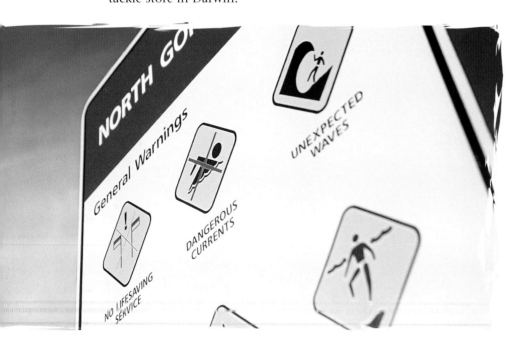

'Matt, when you get to Darwin you've gotta call in and see George and Ronny. Tell 'em I sent ya, mate. We've been friends for over 35 years and not only are they top blokes, they cook the best seafood pasta on earth.'

With a recommendation like that, how could I not call in and say g'day?

Like all people of the North, their generosity and hospitality were outstanding. Ronnie's enthusiasm for fishing (not to mention mine!) found us in a

tinnie the same day I called to meet him in the tackle shop. A 4 a.m. wake-up call the following morning saw us out again. Every day some spectacular fishing adventure happened.

You don't become one of the leading presenters on Channel 9's 'Getaway' without a hunch! Ben was right. I had become that fishing junkie.

George, on the other hand, was waiting for us at home and, with the raps John had given his pasta, man, were we hungry! What a menu of seafood, with his prawn and scallop skewers done on a barbecue being one of George's specialties.

Some serious eating followed!

There's something about the water that really stimulates the appetite. Whether I am surfing, swimming, fishing, just walking along the beachfront or sitting in a restaurant beside the sea, I just want to eat!

# Prawn and scallop skewers

These skewers are very simple but that is usually the best way to appreciate good fresh ingredients. Serve with rice and/or salad for a meal, or as a starter before a more substantial seafood dish.

1 kg green prawns
500 g scallop meat
½ cup (125 ml) olive oil
2 limes, quartered

Soak 12 wooden skewers in cold water for about 30 minutes before you start. This prevents them burning on the BBQ.

Peel the prawns, and leave the tails on if you like. Thread the prawns and scallops onto the skewers, alternating as you go.

Brush with olive oil and put onto a hot BBQ plate. Cook for about 1½ minutes each side, until the flesh changes colour and is just cooked. Be careful not to overcook.

Remove from the heat and squeeze lime juice over. Serve immediately.

MAKES **12** SKEWERS

# Roy's calamari

This must be the most expensive calamari in the world! It cost me a brand new Yamaha four-stroke motor, a Haines Hunter 'family heirloom' boat, twenty grand worth of Shimano fishing gear, and another ten grand of sound equipment – radio and depth sounders!

The day started with Roy (Andrew Symonds), Trent Butler, who was a sales rep for Mossops' Fishing and Tackle, and I setting out from North Stradbroke Island to go fishing in search of some squid and the elusive snapper off the shallow reefs. But it ended with us swimming for our lives for more than an hour, sometimes through the middle of schools of bait fish, which are notorious feeding grounds for sharks.

There would have been 150 people standing around watching at Amity Point when our vessel, after being swamped in Moreton Bay, was salvaged. It was as if the trip had turned into a near national disaster! I'm certainly not suggesting it was a world-shattering story. However, the news did reach as far as the UK and India. To this day it remains a frequently asked question during press conferences all over the world. It was embarrassing, but at least we had our lives.

The thing about our fishing is that we like to get out on our fishing grounds at first light. No matter what type of fish we're chasing, light is crucial. First light or last light is your best chance, regardless of the moon and tide times. At the height of a Queensland summer, the sun is up and across the water at 4 a.m. We were out before sunrise and were sitting on the bar that runs alongside North Stradbroke Island. There was a dropping easterly swell. The plan was to cross the bar as soon as there was enough light.

Then it happened! We almost got out through the bar when we were hit pretty hard by a wave we didn't see until too late. It came down heavily and buried the back of the boat in the water. The motor cut out! I ran down to the back of the boat to see if the battery had been dislodged and – *wham*! – another wave hit us. Hard! And then we were right in the impact zone. That last wave turned the boat on its side and then – *bang*! – the next wave! The cabin was half filled with water in the blink of an eye. Our life jackets and our EPERB emergency beacon were going under, along with our hope.

Without wasting words, and with a ton of burley washing into the ocean with us, I said, 'Boys, we're swimming!' None of us wanted to be shark bait!

In the rush, we didn't even have time to put on our life jackets, but I managed to stuff my beloved sunglasses down my Speedos. We left everything, jumped off the back of the boat and started swimming with the current because there was absolutely no point fighting it. The current was taking us along the shoreline and we were about 1 kilometre off the mainland. I reckoned we had about 40 minutes of swimming in front of us.

I knew Simmo was a strong swimmer and I knew I was. We didn't know about Trent though, but he started off doing freestyle and that was a good sign. When I asked him if he could swim, he replied, 'I'm no Kieren Perkins, mate, but I reckon I go all right.' Under the circumstances, I took the fact that he could come up with a reply even half witty as a good sign.

But then, after about 20 minutes into it, Trent said, 'Mate, I'm gone.' He was exhausted.

I said to him that I could swim back towards the boat, where the professional fishermen were starting to run their search patterns and alert them, or we would swim on with him doing sidestroke. I gave him a moment or two to reflect on his decision then I said, 'What do you reckon, mate, what's the go?'

'Yep, I can do it,' he said and we swam on.

We went through bait-fish schools of pilchards on several occasions but, honestly, the last thing I was thinking about was getting eaten by a shark. I was more worried about Trent and whether or not we could get him over the line.

As we approached the shore, there was another break, a lull, and then the beach break. We got across the outer bank okay and were able to stand up briefly, but then we had to swim again and Trent had no energy.

'Come on, mate, you can stand up,' Simmo encouraged.

'Just one final big push and we're home sweet home, champ.' I urged. Off we went again.

Exhaustion overcame Trent. The stress, combined with the gruelling swim, finally reached breaking point with him. Truly, he was spent like a salmon at the end of its spawning run.

Taking one arm each, Simmo and I dragged him home to safety.

Flopping down like a scene out of 'Gilligan's Island', the three of us took a moment to take stock of what had just happened. Not only were we all safe but somehow I'd managed to save my favourite old sunnies.

Suddenly Simmo burst into laughter. 'Hey, have a look at this muppet,' Simmo said to Trent. 'Look at Haydos. He's got his sunnies on. He's bloody salvaged his sunnies!'

'Eyes and teeth, mate. God only gives you one crack at 'em!' I retorted jokingly.

At the end of the day it was a time for humour. We all still had our lives.

This is a great opportunity to express my appreciation to all those who helped in any way, especially the Volunteer Rescue Service. Congratulations on the job you do for the waterways of Australia. You're all champion Australians.

# Roy's calamari

4 tablespoons butter
½ small onion, finely chopped
4 cloves garlic, finely chopped
3 teaspoons curry powder
500 g squid tubes, washed and sliced into rings
1 lime, halved

Melt the butter in a frying pan. Add the onion and garlic and cook until soft and lightly browned. Add the curry powder and cook, stirring, for 30 seconds. Transfer to a large mixing bowl and leave to cool.

When the mixture is cool add the calamari. Stir to coat well, then cover and put in the fridge to marinate for about 30 minutes.

Heat a BBQ plate until very hot and throw on the calamari. Cook for 2–3 minutes, until the calamari changes colour, tossing regularly.

Put onto a serving plate and squeeze lime juice over. Serve straight away.

SERVES 6–8 AS A STARTER

# Seafood gumbo

The northern Queensland outpost of Cooktown was the scene of one of my great fishing flops. Yet, just 45 minutes south, it was the scene of one of my great fishing triumphs. Fishing can be fickle like that.

Andrew Symonds and I were in the north on the beautiful Endeavour River on which Cooktown stands. We were definitely 'two fish out of our water'! We had fished the river hard for seven days and caught just three fish.

We had tried all the different locations, all the right baits and, believe me, had asked all the right people all the right questions.

'Ah, mate, ya shoulda been 'ere yesterday, 'eh,' we were told. But today it was deathly quiet!

There's a saying in North Queensland fishing circles: 'No Run. No Fun.' And there was no tidal run in the Endeavour River because there was no moon. The tides were really neap. It was hot, very hot, and we were tucked up on the mangroves being eaten alive by sandflies, dodging crocs and making pathetic excuses for why it just wasn't happening for us. If we had not been such good mates, we would have strangled each other!

So on the seventh day, we left for a small community 45 minutes south called Archer Point. We set up camp on the beach, just opposite an unnamed island where the grave of a lone sailor lies. (Perhaps he wasn't catching fish either!) Our tinnie had no depth sounder, so we threw the anchor out and if we hooked upon the reef, we cast out.

Then it happened! I yelled excitedly but slowly, as I spat the sixth-day dummy out at the same time, 'We're into 'em, mate!'

Simmo gave his usual snuffle and rub of the nose and said, 'Yeah! 'Bout bloody time!' Then we were running hot. Fish everywhere!

I couldn't believe it! Within 15 minutes I was sick of catching fish. I started filleting them and throwing their backbones over the side. But they were barely hitting the water as Spanish mackerel smashed into them. They were absolute horses! We had plenty of fun on those mackerel for an hour.

And then there were the queenfish. There must have been three acres of queenfish and none was less than 10 kilos. Every time we threw in, we got a fish. It didn't rain, but it poured fish. We really needed that. We had been struggling for so long on the good old Endeavour River.

Just as we had become frustrated not catching fish at Cooktown, we were almost frustrated catching fish off Archer Point! The trip was so good! All the effort we went to and could not catch a fish; then, barely trying, we were catching fish after fish. That night we lit the campfire on the beach and talked lies all night!

SEAFOOD

# Seafood gumbo

2 tablespoons peanut oil

1 large onion, chopped

1 large red capsicum, chopped

1 large green capsicum, chopped

2 garlic cloves, crushed

1 teaspoon ground cumin

½ teaspoon ground allspice

½ teaspoon cayenne pepper

2 x 400g cans diced tomatoes

1 cup (250 ml) fish or chicken stock

2 bay leaves

2 teaspoons thyme leaves

100 g okra, halved lengthways (optional)

500 g green prawns, peeled and deveined

150 g scallop meat

500 g firm white fish fillets, such as ling

Gumbo is a spicy stew which comes from Louisiana in southern USA. It is based on tomatoes and capsicums, and to be authentic would include okra. This can be hard to find, so leave it out if you have to — it will still taste great. Serve with rice to soak up the sauce.

Heat the oil in a large saucepan and add the onion and capsicum. Cook over medium heat for a few minutes, until soft. Add the garlic and spices and cook for 1 minute, stirring. Add the tomatoes, stock, bay leaves, thyme and okra, and simmer, uncovered, for 10 minutes.

Add the seafood to the pan and bring back to the boil. Reduce the heat so the mixture is just simmering and cook for about 5 minutes, stirring occasionally, until the seafood is cooked. Serve with rice.

SERVES 4–6

# Nola's chicken pie

It's funny the direction life takes you when you follow your instincts.

The first time I came off the Gabba – back in 1991, my debut – I had made 149 against South Australia and there was this little fella yelling out, 'Matty! Matty! Matty!' I knew I couldn't speak to him then, but as I walked into the dressing room I can remember thinking, 'I reckon I'll go back and have a bit of a chat with that little shaver. He looked a really decent kid!'

After having a shower, I brought my gear up to air it in the sun and then went over to this little bloke and asked him his name.

He was Bart, 10 years old, and he looked me excitedly in the eyes and asked, 'Please sign my bat?'

As a young 'un, good manners were really stressed by my parents and, without hesitation, I said to him, 'With pleasure.' I asked him where he was from and he told me Coolum, on the Sunshine Coast of Queensland.

He went on, 'I hear you love surfing, Mr Hayden. Why don't you drive up and come for a surf with me and my family?'

His parents, Nola and Mick Wilson, heard this and laughed, but something instinctively told me they were really good people and I would certainly be very welcome. Bart, handing me a pencil and paper, said, 'Here's our address.'

With laughter in the background, I took down Bart's address.

A few weeks later, I headed to the Sunshine Coast and, again instinctively, decided to look them up. To this day they are some of my best friends. Bart was page boy at our wedding.

Young Bart has grown up now, along with his brothers, Julian and Seb. Julian is one of the best surfers in the world, contracted by a major surfing company. And Seb and Bart are Australian long-board champions and compete internationally.

They have this house at Coolum and when you walk into it you get an amazing feeling. You sense the walls would not be standing but for the blue tac and glue holding the photos on. There are pics of the boys growing up, surfing, and some with me and my girls. It's really wonderful!

Nola said Bart always gravitated towards me. There was a real connection. One day, when he was young, he had written me a birthday card and was hoping to see me at the Gabba to give it to me. After batting,

I must have stayed under the grandstand and, apparently, he was so disappointed that he cried. Nola then told him to put the card under the windscreen of my car. I'll never forget that birthday card. It was really appreciated.

Meeting the Wilsons taught me a lesson that if you open your eyes to people it's amazing who you can meet. As a sportsman, I'm privileged to travel all around the world, but it doesn't take much to give someone a moment of your time. I did that with Bart and, for me, it opened up a wonderfully generous family.

Her kindness aside, Nola's other great attribute is her Chicken pie. Believe me, after spending hours in the surf, all you want to do is eat, and Nola makes this massive chicken pie that feeds the five of us – and after surfing, I am usually as hungry as ten men! It is an old-fashioned classic that fits the bill perfectly after rolling around in the surf and the sand for hours on end.

CHICKEN

# Nola's chicken pie

1 whole BBQ chicken
1 tablespoon butter
1 onion, chopped
100 g button mushrooms, halved and sliced
1 tablespoon plain flour
½ cup (125 ml) milk
½ cup (125 ml) chicken stock
1 cup (150 g) frozen peas, thawed
2 hard-boiled eggs, quartered
375 g block frozen puff pastry, thawed
milk, to brush

Preheat the oven to 190°C.

Pull the meat from the chicken and tear into bite-sized pieces; set aside. Melt the butter in a frying pan and cook the onion until soft. Add the mushrooms and cook until they are just soft.

Sprinkle the flour over the onion mixture and cook, stirring, for about 30 seconds.

Gradually add the combined milk and stock, stirring constantly. Bring to the boil, then reduce the heat and simmer for 3 minutes.

Stir the chicken and the peas into the sauce. Spoon into a 4-cup capacity pie dish (with a lip) and arrange the egg quarters into the mixture.

Roll out the pastry so that it is about 3 cm bigger than the pie dish. Cut long strips (about 1 cm wide) from the pastry and press onto the lip of the dish. Wipe a little water onto the pastry strips with your fingers.

Lay the remaining pastry over the dish. Trim the overhanging pastry with a small sharp knife, and press the edges with a fork to seal. Brush lightly with milk, and prick some holes in the top. Bake for 30 minutes, until the pastry is golden brown.

SERVES 6

# crispy chicken

Crispy chicken has its origins in North Queensland – a location that is a favourite playground of mine with its national parks, Atherton Tableland lakes, beautiful islands, beaches and spectacular Great Barrier Reef. There's something really special about the north. My brother, Gary, lives there on the coast near Ingham, with his wife, Alex, and their children. We have spent hours marauding around the countryside, fishing, hunting pigs and riding horses – though Gary is no horseman!

Once Gary and I were riding along Forrest Beach when he came unstuck and ended up with a mouthful of sand. The horse had merely gone from a walk to a trot!

Concerned locals moved towards him, checking and inquiring about his wellbeing, to which Gary replied, 'I'm fine. Just breaking the horse in.' The truth of the matter was the horse was 15 years old and as timid as they come!

That coastal region, about 100 kilometres north of Townsville, is a glorious place where a cooling wind blows continuously off the ocean. No better climate exists in their so-called 'winter' months! It's a great place for just getting back to nature. Gary reckons that when I get up there, put on my weather-worn old hat and go unshaven, I look like Jungle Jim.

Gary and Alex used to live in a shack right on the beach at a place called Cassidy Beach. Recently, a woman was walking along that beach and thought she spied a log ahead in the sand – only to see it grow legs and scurry into the water! Another woman was driving at night towards a nearby town called Lucinda when she saw a 2-metre crocodile on the road ahead. Locals in this region have learned to just live with crocs.

It was at the Cassidy Beach shack that Alex relayed messages to Gary regarding my first-ever Test century against the West Indies. Gary was windsurfing, too nervous to watch the television, and asked his wife to use different coloured towels to signal my progress towards the 100.

The shack had great atmosphere. Its location and views, too, were spectacular. You had the impression, though, that great damage could be done to it, especially by winds associated with North Queensland's cyclonic weather! A recent cyclone was the reason Gary, Alex and their three children moved to a safer location.

Crispy chicken is actually a dish that Alex once cooked for us and, like many dishes, has been tasted, enjoyed and prepared again and again. That Alex was able to weave her magic in the shack's very limited kitchen and conjure up quality meals, like crispy chicken, remains a credit to her.

When I first went up there to visit, Alex used to feed me what Gary ate. She is a great cook but Gary loves his creamy dishes and pasta and, especially when I'm in training, I need to watch my diet. Kell keeps me on track with this when I am at home. I can hear her saying in answer to questions about food, 'We have learned that we have to watch what Matt eats because he is in training.'

The pasta and creamy dishes are gone from the menu when I am in town, but crispy chicken has stood the test of time.

# Crispy chicken

2 cups (500 ml) soy sauce

¾ cup (185 ml) sherry

3 cups (750 ml) water

1 onion, finely chopped

1 tablespoon chopped fresh ginger

½ cup (100 g) brown sugar

1 whole chicken (no. 18)

This chicken is beautiful served with roast vegies in winter, or a salad in summer.

Put the soy sauce, sherry, water, onion, ginger and sugar into a very large pot. Stir over medium heat to dissolve the sugar, then bring to the boil. Turn the heat down to low. Tuck the chicken wings under the body and put the chicken into the liquid, breast side down.

Simmer gently for 30 minutes. Preheat the oven to 180°C.

Carefully lift the chicken from the pan and place breast side up on a wire rack in a baking pan. Cook in the oven for 30 minutes, until the skin is crisp.

SERVES 4

# Kell's asparagus chicken casserole

There are times when the plane is coming in to land at Brisbane airport after an overseas or interstate tour that I swear I can smell Kell's asparagus chicken casserole cooking in the oven! This is my favourite dish made with love from my favourite girl. It was also the first-ever dish she made for me when we met.

Before I even met her, Kell always cooked it for her parents and two brothers. Kell learned to cook the dish at school in Year 10 during a Home Economics class, and over the years she has really perfected it. Because she knew it so well, she had the confidence to cook it for me during the early stages of our courting. It has been a winner ever since!

When we are touring Australia and Kell is travelling with me, it is an easy dish for her to make, a meal where everything gets thrown in.

Kell's asparagus chicken casserole is so popular. Good things are meant to be shared, especially with family, so her recipe has now gone 1500 kilometres up to North Queensland to my brother, Gary. He loves good food, too, so his insistence on having the recipe for Kell's dish speaks for itself.

Kell is a really good cook. Simple is best with her. And, more than anything, our love of food has been one of the key ingredients for our life in marriage. It is something we share and do well together. Just sitting around the kitchen in the evening, preparing a meal, is one of the highlights of our day.

When we travel, one thing we really love doing is experiencing eating in different places, be it in Venice or Brisbane. But having said that, there is nothing quite like a simple home-cooked meal and Kell does that fabulously, with her Asparagus chicken casserole at the top of the list.

CHICKEN

# Kell's asparagus chicken casserole

½ cup (75 g) plain flour
salt and pepper
4 chicken breast or thigh fillets
1 tablespoon olive oil
1 teaspoon butter
1 onion, finely diced
2 garlic cloves, crushed
6 button mushrooms, thickly sliced
2 x 400 g cans cream of asparagus soup
juice of 1 lemon

Chicken thighs are more flavoursome than breast fillets, but are higher in fat.
Serve this dish with steamed vegetables and steamed basmati rice, if you like.

Preheat the oven to 180°C.

Cut each of the fillets into three pieces. Combine the flour, salt and pepper on a plate. Dust the chicken with the seasoned flour, shaking off the excess.

Heat the oil and butter in a frying pan and add the onion and garlic. Cook until soft and brown, then remove from the pan leaving behind the oil and butter.

Add the chicken to the pan and cook until well browned.

Place the chicken into a large casserole dish along with the onion mixture and the mushrooms.

Pour the soup and lemon juice over the chicken. Cover and bake for 45 minutes.

SERVES 4

# Chicken curry

It goes without saying that on a cricket tour to the subcontinent, when I walk into a kitchen to watch a chef make a meal, it blows the staff's minds away! The kitchenhands are infatuated, and incredibly surprised, that a cricketer, let alone a well-known cricketer, is sharing their workspace with them. It just shocks them! When I walk into their kitchen there is a hush. The chef and assistants all try to get on with their business, and they are very attentive to their jobs, but I can feel my presence is creating great interest. There is the odd whisper and an occasional voice can be heard.

Sri Lanka is the more laidback part of the subcontinent. There is much less hustle and bustle than in India. Like Indians, Sri Lankans are not loud-speaking. Their voices do not boom out and dominate the streets. But in India, it is considered good luck to touch the fortunate, so the Indians are much more tactile than Sri Lankans.

There is no problem with your safety. Indians are not aggressive, but when they see you, you feel like The Beatles must have felt. It is like Beatlemania! For a country boy, it blows me away that I have that type of impact on people. By contrast, the Sri Lankans tend to look from afar. And so they did this evening in the hotel we were staying at, when I enjoyed the enlightening experience of learning the subtle touches of making a curry from a local chef.

Curry on the subcontinent is considered a status symbol. If a potential wife can make a curry, it is considered such a gift that it can be included in a bride's dowry.

I said to this chef from the hotel, 'If I learn nothing else tonight, I don't mind. Just as long as I'm taught how to make a good fluffy rice, I'll be more than happy.' What a joy it was for me to mix with those people, become one with them and learn from them.

Because rice is the staple diet of billions of people, it is a critical part of life in any home in the region. Like we have bread, they have rice. Like we have sandwiches, they have soft, fluffy rice that can come fried or sweetened with fruits in it. A typical rice meal might be served with two curries, a form of bread and a kind of coconut sambal, a spicy sauce and some chutneys. It is a busy meal that you eat with your hands.

But rice is the foundation of any meal, and it was a joy to stand at the coalface with these delightful, polite Sri Lankan chefs and kitchen staff and learn the way to cook the dish that is responsible for keeping billions of people satisfied with food in their stomachs.

CHICKEN

2 tablespoons ground coriander

2 teaspoons sweet paprika

2 teaspoons curry powder (see below)

2 teaspoons salt

1 teaspoon chilli powder

½ teaspoon ground turmeric

pinch ground cloves

pinch ground cardamom

6 chicken thigh cutlets

3 teaspoons vegetable oil

1 onion, finely chopped

3 garlic cloves, crushed

1 teaspoon grated fresh ginger

3 curry leaves or bay leaves

1 stalk lemon grass, white part only

2 green chillies, deseeded and
   finely chopped

2 tomatoes, diced

2 cinnamon sticks

1 cup (250 ml) coconut milk

½ cup (125 ml) water

steamed basmati rice, to serve

## Curry Powder

3 tablespoons coriander seeds

3 tablespoons cumin seeds

1½ tablespoons sweet cumin seeds

1 cinnamon stick

10 dried curry leaves

10 cardamom pods

10 cloves

½ teaspoon fenugreek seeds

½ teaspoon yellow mustard seeds

1 tablespoon rice, washed and drained

1 tablespoon desiccated coconut

¼ teaspoon grated nutmeg

# Chicken curry

Making your own curry powder might seem like a chore, but believe me, it's well worth the effort.

Combine the coriander, paprika, curry powder, salt, chilli powder, turmeric, cloves and cardamom. Rub all over the chicken, cover the chicken with plastic wrap and refrigerate for 4 hours.

Heat the oil in a large saucepan and cook the onion until soft and brown. Add the garlic, ginger, curry leaves, lemon grass, chilli, tomato and cinnamon sticks and cook over low heat for 3 minutes, stirring regularly.

Add the chicken, cover and cook over medium heat for 5 minutes. Add the coconut milk and water, bring slowly to boil and simmer for 20 minutes. Take out the cinnamon sticks, lemon grass and bay leaves before serving.

Serve with rice.

SERVES 4–6

To make the curry powder, place all the ingredients in sequence into a dry frying pan over medium heat. Cook, stirring, until well browned and fragrant, but take care not to burn. Leave to cool, then grind to a fine powder. Store in an airtight container in the freezer for up to 1 year.

# Macadamia and feta stuffed chicken

When Kell was pregnant with Grace, her favourite meal was Macadamia and feta stuffed chicken (though at the time, I made it without feta). Just as Kell loves making her Asparagus chicken because she knows it's a favourite of mine, I love cooking her her favourite meal, too. Kell was off her food during her pregnancy and, in desperation, I made this dish for her one night. She loved it!

As blokes, I guess we just don't understand the hardship endured by women during pregnancy – there are some smells and tastes which could not be less enticing. So I kept it simple. I stuffed the meat with English spinach, toasted pinenuts and herbs – not too hard on the old tummy – and avoided garlic and feta, both no-no's during Kell's pregnancy.

While the dish started out simple enough – not too rich – after little Gracey was born and we were relaxing back on Stradbroke Island, the recipe evolved and I started getting more adventurous with the stuffing.

It's always fascinating to hear pregnancy tales, especially those related to food and cravings – the different experiences that make individual pregnancies so unique. Good food and milk were always on the menu with Kell's pregnancy and this dish is now one of Grace's favourites, too. Pregnancy and childbirth are truly a miracle. Fatherhood is a blessing!

CHICKEN

# Macadamia and feta stuffed chicken

⅓ cup (50 g) sesame seeds

2 tablespoons olive oil

1 onion, finely chopped

2 bacon rashers, finely chopped

3 garlic cloves, crushed

200 g feta, chopped

⅓ cup (50 g) macadamias, very finely chopped

2 teaspoons chopped fresh thyme

2 teaspoons chopped fresh rosemary

salt and pepper

4 chicken breast fillets

You could use marinated feta in this recipe to create a slightly different flavour. A 350 g jar of marinated feta will give you about 200 g of feta after draining.

Preheat the oven to 180°C. Place the sesame seeds into a dry frying pan and cook over medium heat, stirring occasionally, for 5 minutes, until golden brown. Transfer to a plate to cool.

Heat half the olive oil in a frying pan and cook the onion, bacon and garlic until lightly browned. Transfer to a large bowl, and cool.

Add the feta, macadamias, sesame seeds and herbs to the onion mixture, and season to taste. Mix with your hands to form a paste.

Cut each chicken fillet in half lengthways horizontally, to make long flat steaks.

Divide the mixture between each piece of chicken, placing it in the centre. Roll the chicken around the stuffing and secure with a toothpick.

Place on an oven tray, brush with remaining olive oil and bake for 25 minutes, until cooked through.

SERVES 4

# Smoked ham and pumpkin soup

An unknown fact about my world record-breaking 380 in Perth in 2003 was how a good old-fashioned serving of Smoked ham and pumpkin soup sustained me as an evening meal.

I had been in Perth for a week prior to the first Test against Zimbabwe. When in Perth, my body clock always seems to be constantly recovering because of the two-hour time difference. So the way I was feeling, a light meal at night really hit the spot for me.

Early days into my stay at the Hyatt Hotel, I ordered this Smoked ham and pumpkin soup that came with the freshest of bread rolls. As the week progressed, I got more and more into that soup. I had it almost every day during my Perth stay. This speaks for itself, given that I felt good enough and had enough energy to bat for 10½ hours. I just liked the way the soup made me feel. It was just enough and I really enjoyed this food in what was an amazing week for me.

People think a cricketer's day is over when he walks off the field. But you have to stretch, have physiotherapy and, at times, even a massage. I had a really sore back at the time and would receive physiotherapy for an hour after each day's play. Then I would have a massage for an hour. By the time I returned to my room, it was nine o'clock at night. I certainly wasn't on fire after that; all I wanted to do was simply crash out. I was just cooked! The last thing I wanted to do was go out to eat. So I stayed in, with my Smoked ham and pumpkin soup.

I love soup at the best of times – from a clear soup, to a thick, stodgy one. It is especially good in the cold winter months. I enjoy that type of eating. It makes you full, but not too full.

Butter and cream are not always necessary in soup – it can easily be lightened with yoghurt, which is a healthy alternative, too. The Hyatt's soup during my stay was just perfect! Having it each night had nothing to do with superstition – it just made me feel right. And the rest is history.

I hope you enjoy my interpretation of this delicious soup.

MEAT

1.5 kg butternut pumpkin, peeled and chopped

300 g potatoes, peeled and chopped

2 teaspoons olive oil

1 small onion, finely chopped

2 garlic cloves, crushed

1 teaspoon chopped rosemary

100 g smoked ham, diced

1 cup (250 ml) chicken stock

salt and pepper

3 tablespoons milk

1 teaspoon butter

4 slices prosciutto, grilled until crisp

extra virgin olive oil, to drizzle

2 teaspoons chopped parsley

# Smoked ham and pumpkin soup

A cold night, some good company, and this delicious soup slides right down.

Cook the pumpkin and potatoes in a large saucepan of boiling salted water until soft.

Meanwhile, heat the oil and cook the onion, garlic and rosemary in a frying pan until soft and lightly golden.

Drain the pumpkin and potato, then place the pumpkin and half the potato into a food processor or blender along with the onion mixture, diced ham and stock. Blend until thick and creamy. Season to taste, and transfer to a saucepan to reheat.

Put the rest of the potato into a bowl and add the milk and butter. Mash until creamy, and season with salt and pepper to taste.

Ladle the soup into serving bowls and add a dollop of mash to the middle. Top with the grilled prosciutto, drizzle with extra virgin olive oil and sprinkle with parsley.

SERVES 4

# Grandma's shepherd's pie

My life growing up in the country is full of rich, wonderful memories that time shall never diminish. One such memory is enjoying the love and attention of my grandparents in Kingaroy, and the wondrous cooking of my beloved Grandma.

After my dad purchased our property from Grandma and Pop, they relocated to live in a fairly central part of Kingaroy, within close walking distance to school and church. Every Sunday we would all go to Mass and then on to Grandma and Pop's place where a Sunday roast was a tradition.

Sunday lunch was very much a part of Australian bush culture. It was the one time in the week when a family was able to sit down and spend quality time together. After lunch, too, was special. Visitors and relatives would drop in and either chat with Mum and Grandma or play billiards with Pop and Dad. The kids would play cricket with one of the next-door neighbours or, when we were tall enough to put our noses over the billiard table and hold a cue, join in with Pop and Dad. Everyone would eagerly await afternoon tea, and Grandma's malted milks are still rave material!

During the week Dad would be out working on the property and Mum, a teacher, would be at school, sometimes working after school helping students, going to staff meetings or doing extracurricular activities like producing and directing school musicals.

Our very early cricket years were spent playing Junior Cricket. This was mainly played on Saturday mornings, so Sunday was a grand gathering.

I remember Grandma always had leftovers from the Sunday roast dinner, that were ground up in an old-style hand mincer. It didn't matter what type of roast meat was left over – pork, lamb, beef. It was a very, very simple way to make the roast extend for another two lunches during the week – or even for smoko for the farmhands, in earlier times. Grandma would put the minced-up meat into a baking dish, put mashed potato on top and bake it until it was a golden brown on top. It was a great feed!

I had a great relationship with my grandparents. One of the greatest things you can do is enjoy the love of grandparents. I was very fortunate with my grandparents, on both sides of our family. It is so important and such a beautiful part of a child's development because, I believe, while it is a parent's job to discipline children, it is a grandparent's job to spoil them with love.

So much wisdom comes from older people, who are often ready and willing to invest time in people's lives, and kids are 'sponges' for that. Grandma and Pop spoiled my brother, Gary, and myself. Pop would tell me intriguing stories about the land, and every afternoon I would go to his house, which was only seconds from the school, to wait for Mum to finish work. Some days I would even go there for lunch and that was always a treat.

Grandma would spoil us rotten! I didn't have vegemite sandwiches for lunch. It would be a three-course meal!

Grandma and Pop grew everything in their garden – lettuce, carrots, beans, peas, potatoes – vegetables of all kinds! Peach trees, in season, had their branches fully burdened with huge, juicy, delicious fruit and their grapes tasted just so good. Chutney was made from tomatoes and various home-grown fruits, and Grandma's jams, made from figs, strawberries, gooseberries, mulberries, oranges, or any other fruit that was in season, were always a treat, especially on hot scones or pikelets.

The chookhouse, too, had its place! Fresh eggs were always added to other ingredients and whisked up into some magical culinary delights. Many a chook ate up well, only to be beheaded, plucked and cleaned and then cooked and eaten heartily!

They were different days and it is sad as they are kind of 'lost' days.

It meant so much to me as a kid to have grandparents in my life. I believe that through their love, care, kindness and the traditions they passed on, I have been given great gifts and am determined never to lose them. It was a wonderful thing, knowing how much my grandparents loved me and how much, in return, they also were loved.

So that's why I have put Grandma's shepherd's pie in this book. It is part of my tradition, my memories, and I want to keep them always.

600 g cooked roast lamb

1 cup (250 ml) beef stock

2 teaspoons cornflour or arrowroot

salt and pepper

2 teaspoons olive oil

2 onions, halved and finely sliced

4 tomatoes, finely sliced

1 kg potatoes, peeled and chopped

¼ cup (60 ml) milk

2 tablespoons butter

# Grandma's shepherd's pie

Shepherd's pie is traditionally made from lamb, but you could also use leftover roast beef.

Preheat the oven to 180°C.

Mince the meat in a food processor, or an old-fashioned hand-operated mincer if you have one. Place into an 8-cup capacity baking dish.
Mix the beef stock with the cornflour, and season with salt and pepper. Pour over the mince.

Heat the oil in a frying pan and cook the onions until soft and lightly browned. Layer the onions and tomatoes over the mince.

Meanwhile, boil the potatoes until tender. Drain well then mash with the milk, butter and a pinch of salt. Spoon the mash over the top of the filling to form a thick crust. Bake for about 45 minutes, until golden brown.

SERVES 6

# South African braai (BBQ)

If ever there was a carnivorous race, it's the South Africans. When you go to a restaurant in South Africa and order a steak, half a beast comes delivered to you on a plate. You don't feel dissimilar to Fred Flintstone after he pulls away from the American Diner. Like the Americans, South Africans have big meals. In Australia, we love putting steak on the barbecue, burning it, then smothering it in tomato sauce before throwing it on a bread roll. But in South Africa, they are masters of marinating their meat, which enables them to cut down their cooking time and infuse delicious flavours into the meat. They are famous, too, for their sausages: boerewors.

Because the country has such rich grazing land, the quality of their meat and the way they prepare it is second to none.

Meat while on safari is truly supreme! It is part of the South African experience to get out in the bush, light a big fire and sit under the African skies. Then, when the fire dies down a bit, lie out a grill across it and cook meat that has been marinated for a long time.

The bush is an amazing place in South Africa. It is truly the great outdoors. I have been fortunate enough to have enjoyed some extraordinary safari experiences in Africa. One of the best was witnessing the migration of wildebeest across the plains. As these wildebeest reached the river crossings, there were crocodiles just basking in the sun or sitting there, still as logs, waiting to pounce on their fresh prey and drag them into the depths of the water. South Africa can be such a wild, unforgiving country!

In the morning, you rise before the sun and watch lions prepare for a vicious kill. You are on edge the whole time. You are in a car, but you are watching life unfold so incredibly close to you. The pecking order is well and truly established in that place!

In the evening, as the sun dips and the stars take over, it is a really special experience. Because South Africa is in the same hemisphere as Australia, the same stars can be seen. The Southern Cross is so striking in the sky.

Fire, with its warmth and feather-like flames, is a captivator. Those around it are drawn in, almost hypnotically, and beckoned to tell stories of truth, home and culture, and culinary delights are soon exposed. Like a moth is attracted to light so, too, are those around the fire enticed to talk.

# South African braai (BBQ)

2 kg whole piece rump
1 garlic clove
2 (500 ml) cups red wine
½ cup (125 ml) olive oil
1 onion, chopped
4 bacon rashers, chopped
¼ cup (60 ml) soy sauce
2 cups (500 ml) BBQ sauce (smoky flavour)
10 large sprigs of fresh rosemary

*You could serve this with couscous salad or pesto pasta salad. Tomato, mozzarella and basil salad is also a favourite.*

Put the meat into a large glass or ceramic dish. Lay the side of a large knife blade on the garlic clove and flatten with the heel of your hand. Combine with the remaining ingredients (except the rosemary) and pour over the meat. Cover with plastic wrap and leave in the fridge for at least half a day, or up to 24 hours.

Drain the meat and reserve the marinade. Sear each side on a moderately hot BBQ plate. Turn the heat down to low, cover and cook for 2 hours. (I love the Weber or any BBQ with a lid to prevent meat from drying out during cooking. If you don't have one, you can cover the meat with foil.)

During this time, place the rosemary sprigs on the heat diffusers on the BBQ. This smokes and permeates the meat giving it an amazing flavour. Baste occasionally with leftover marinade.

Rest the meat for 15 minutes, before slicing to serve.

SERVES 6–8

# Bangers and mash

This is a tribute to the grandparents of my wife, Kellie, and something to silence my Australian team-mate, Jason 'Dizzy' Gillespie. When I was talking with the boys, telling them I was doing a cookbook, an avalanche of rubbishing almost buried me.

Yet, when the dust settled and their attempted humour subsided, Dizzy said one thing was an absolute must for the book: 'You have to have bangers and mash in there, because you can't be an Australian without enjoying bangers and mash.'

When I first met Kell, the West Indies team was touring Australia, and Queensland was scheduled to play a match against them in Bundaberg. Kell thought it was an ideal chance for us to catch up with her grandparents who lived in the centre of good old Bundy.

Every morning delicious smells would waft by, as Kell's granddad cooked the best bangers and mash in town. It was a morning ritual. Kell's grandmother would go to daily Mass and her granddad would make you a cuppa, black with no sugar, like a good old bushie. Whichever grandchildren were visiting at the time would also bound out of bed and join in the tasty tradition of visiting the local baker

for fresh bread, and then popping into the newsagent for the *'Bundy' Times*. Then came the big breakfast.

As for most people of that generation, breakfast was a massive meal. It was kind of like the No.1 meal of the day. Well, Kell's granddad upheld that tradition! He would put these sausages in a tub of oil and fry the hell out of them. And then he would drain a little bit of oil out and make rich brown gravy. It was so nice, I can still taste it today!

In addition, he would make sure that before he cooked the breakfast, he went to the local bakery and bought a loaf of high-top white bread. He would cut slabs off the bread and dip into the gravy. What a feed! There we were, at 6.30 a.m., drinking black tea out of old teacups and eating bangers and mash.

Like all those bushies, he was wafer-thin! He was built like a stickman and had skin like leather, toughened from his years working in the steamy Bundy summer days on the railways. It was not a breakfast for the health conscious! But it was an epic, an old-fashioned treasure, that lives on in the memories of Kell and me.

# Bangers and mash

3 cups (750 ml) beef stock

8 thick pork or beef sausages

2 tablespoons vegetable oil (or roast drippings)

1 tablespoon plain flour

salt and pepper, to taste

1 kg potatoes, peeled and chopped

1 tablespoon butter

3 tablespoons milk

Put the stock into a large saucepan and slowly bring to boil. When it is warm but not yet boiling, add the sausages. When the stock comes to the boil, remove the sausages. Keep the stock aside.

Heat the oil in a frying pan and add the sausages. Cook over medium heat until well browned and cooked through. (It's best to use a frying pan that isn't non-stick, because you want to get the sausages and the pan really brown, which makes a better colour and flavour for the gravy.) Drain the sausages on paper towels.

Return the pan to the heat. Add the flour and stir, scraping the bottom of the pan. Gradually add 2 cups (500 ml) of the reserved stock, stirring constantly to make smooth gravy. Season with salt and pepper to taste.

Meanwhile, cook the potatoes in a large saucepan of boiling water. Drain well, return to the pan and mash until smooth. Stir in the butter and milk, and season to taste.

Serve the bangers and mash with the gravy.

SERVES 4

# Gabby's lasagne

Gracie's favourite meal, Gabby's lasagne, has its roots in a magnificent Italian district that is renowned as the culinary capital of Italy. The town of Ortona, in the Abruzzo district of Italy, is a gloriously beautiful mountainside village wedged up against the seaside. Such is its culinary reputation that Italy's most promising chefs are sent to the town to ply their craft.

Gabby, the mother of our beautiful deceased friend, Daniela, was raised in the Ortona township which, although flattened during World War II, remains overflowing with history.

Now Gabby resides in Brisbane, having followed her husband (coincidentally named Gabriele) from Italy to Queensland in 1965.

They are typically hard-working Italians. Gabriele was a cane cutter at Finch Hatton, west of Mackay, which is a settlement in the Pioneer Valley that leads to the lovely rainforests of Eungella, about 80 kilometres west of the Coral Coast. For six months of the year he would cut cane, and for the other six months he would join Gabby working at the cannery in Brisbane.

Gabby, now a renowned dressmaker, is a person who would do anything for anybody.

Her son-in-law, Kevin, who was married to Daniela, affectionately refers to her as Alice, the character from 'The Brady Bunch', because she will arrive for a visit but end up doing the cleaning and the cooking. If you go away on holidays, she will mow the lawn. She treats Kevin's dogs, Roxy and Heidi, like they are her grandchildren.

Our daughter, Grace, just loves Gabby. She goes to the same church as we do, and Gracie will spend the entire service walking between her mother and Gabby.

Grace gives Gabby great joy and this warms our hearts like we never could have imagined. People ask what is Grace's favourite age for us. 'Every day!' I reply. Why? She makes me laugh so much all the time. She's a real little mimic with her individual sense of humour. Gracie and I have an amazing bond. It doesn't matter whether I've been away for three months or two weeks, when we're back together we're able to pick up where we left off.

She is a wonderful child who has brought great joy to Kell's parents who had to deal with the tragedy of losing their son, Chris, when he was 19.

Gracie calls Kell's mum Mama, and Kell's dad Cookie, because he loves eating cookies with his cup of tea.

I'm sure she also calls Gabby, in her mind at least, the best cook around. Gabby's lasagne is a beauty which Gracie mops up, then comes back for seconds. Our entire family is blessed for the role Gabby plays in all of our lives.

the MATTHEW HAYDEN cookbook

2 tablespoons olive oil

1 onion, finely chopped

2 garlic cloves, crushed

500 g lean beef mince

¼ cup (60 ml) white wine

400 g can whole peeled Roma tomatoes

700 g bottle of Italian tomato sauce (sugo)

2 teaspoons dried Italian herbs

beef or pork bone

large sprig fresh basil, chopped

2 x 250 g boxes instant lasagna sheets

1 teaspoon salt

1 teaspoon olive oil

100 g finely grated Parmesan cheese

100 g grated mild cheese (such as tasty)

100 g grated mozzarella cheese

# Gabby's lasagne

Good on the night but not bad either after having a 'sleep' in the fridge!

Heat the oil in a large saucepan and cook the onion and garlic until soft and lightly brown. Add the mince, breaking it up with a wooden spoon, and cook until all the liquid has evaporated. Add the white wine and cook until evaporated, then add the tomatoes, tomato sauce and herbs.

Add the meat bone and simmer over low heat, partially covered, for 1 hour. Add the basil 15 minutes before the sauce is cooked.

Meanwhile, bring a large pot of water to the boil, add salt and olive oil. Add 4 lasagna sheets, one at a time, and cook for 5 minutes until soft (move with a fork to help keep the sheets separate). Lift out with a large slotted spoon into cold water to stop the cooking process, then drain on a clean cotton table cloth or tea towels. Repeat with remaining lasagna sheets. Preheat the oven to 180°C.

To assemble the lasagne, layer the pasta sheets, meat sauce and combined cheeses in a large (10-cup capacity) lasagne dish. Tuck the top layer of pasta sheets in at the sides, and finish with a thin layer of meat sauce then a topping of the combined cheeses.

Bake for 30 minutes, until the cheese is lightly browned.

SERVES 8

# Traditional spaghetti sauce

I love my family and, in particular, the memories of sitting around sharing great food, wine, jokes and stories. This is part of my tradition. Life just wouldn't be the same without family. Fortunately, I have been privileged to be part of an exclusive, extended family, too – the Australian cricket team family. One that travels, trains, plays and eats together! A family with members who live in each other's pockets for ten-and-a-half months a year.

Talking about eating, one Aussie family member springs immediately to mind. Yes! None other than Merv Hughes whose popular joke is 'I'm on a diet! A seafood diet! I see food – and I eat it!' With such simple criteria in mind, cooking a meal for Merv is always a breeze!

It was in the summer of 1996, perhaps '95, and Queensland played Victoria at the Gabba. Queensland was in mucho trouble by the end of the third day. Dean 'Deano' Jones declared overnight and left us chasing a 300-plus total on the last day.

I had previously organised to host Merv at my home on that particular night. Well, by late afternoon, Merv was on fire! Victoria was on top and Merv just loved rubbing salt into our wounds. In the first innings, I was out for a duck – the big zero – and Merv just couldn't help himself! After the close of play that day, he sneaked into the Queensland dressing room and drew ducks over all my gear, especially my bat, as that was to be my tool of the trade the next morning.

Mum and Dad had travelled down from Kingaroy to watch the match at the Gabba and at the close of play I dashed up to the stands to let my parents know that Merv would be joining us for dinner at home in a short time. I had just phoned Kell and asked her to come as well.

Mum went into panic mode! 'Kell's fine! She's always a joy to have and she's easy to feed, but Merv?' she questioned. 'Matt, you're going to need a horse and a cow to feed him!'

After me telling Mum not to worry and assuring her there was enough food in the house to appease Merv's incredible appetite, Mum turned to Dad and said, 'Well, thank heavens we brought down those three buckets of Grandma's peaches.'

Merv arrived for dinner as chirpy as a bird, very cocky and unbelievably jovial. We all set about creating the 'perfect meal'. I was particularly focused on the fact Merv had to bowl to me early the next morning!

'What have you got here, Haydos? Ah … peaches!' he exclaimed, and he devoured first one bucketful of peaches and then a second.

Now it's important for you to realise that Merv is one of the biggest con artists in the world. His ability to talk someone into doing anything is renowned. I realised he had Mum in mind as his next victim!

'OK, Haydos,' he said as he opened the kitchen cupboards. 'Now, what have we got here? Yep, this'll do, and this, and this, and …' He continued until most of the food was taken from all the cupboards! I joined in, too, till the cupboards were bare.

'We need a really big saucepan. Yep,' he said, satisfied he had found the largest one in the kitchen, as he dipped in to take more peaches from a third bucket. 'Mmmmmmm, these peaches are really delicious!'

Anything and everything was thrown into the saucepan. Then Mum was called into the action while Kell and Dad looked on with interest and perhaps a slight sense of suspicion.

'You'll boil the kettle for me, won't you?' Merv asked Mum sweetly. Mum, at least, knew how to do that! We often tease Mum about her cooking and Merv knew that.

Now, Mum swears this next part of the story didn't happen, but Kell, Dad, Merv and I know it definitely did. Probably the whole of Australia knows now, as Merv uses this story as part of his repartee! He handed Mum a massive fist of spaghetti and asked her to put it into the kettle to cook. Mum was about to do that. Laughing, we all stopped her.

She always denies that story vehemently. 'I wouldn't have done that!' Then quickly concedes, 'Well, if it did happen it's probably because Merv is such a big con artist and, anyway,' she goes on, 'I would have thought, in the nicest possible way mind you, that Merv is a real character and *he probably does boil spaghetti in his kettle!*'

Kell's side of the story is that Mum did it all right, but she knew Merv was playing a trick and just went along with it to be a good sport.

Anyhow, it was a great meal. And the outcome had the desired effect.

Big Merv had to bowl to me first thing the next day. I'll never forget watching Merv as he came in bowling to me the next morning, with his big guts wobbling up and down full of Grandma's peaches and the huge meal he had devoured the previous night.

I believe I have never batted better than that day. The perfect meal produced perfect batting for me. My score was something like 200-plus not out and Queensland won the game just after tea.

Yes! The proof of the pudding is in the eating!

2 tablespoons olive oil or butter

1 large onion, finely chopped

4 garlic cloves, crushed

1 heaped tablespoon finely chopped fresh rosemary

3 or 4 fresh basil leaves, finely chopped (optional)

6 mushrooms, finely chopped

5 skinned chicken giblets, finely chopped (optional)

½ skinned cacciatore salami, finely chopped (optional)

500 g rump, round or topside steak, finely chopped

2 tablespoons tomato paste

400 g can diced tomatoes

pinch mixed spice

salt and pepper, to taste

# Traditional spaghetti sauce

You could leave out the can of tomatoes, but add an extra tablespoon of tomato paste. A small amount of chicken, pork or prosciutto could also be included.

Heat most of the oil or butter (reserve 2 teaspoons) in a frying pan – preferably not a non-stick pan because you want to get a good browning on the bottom of the pan. Add the onion, garlic, rosemary and basil. Cook on low until the onion is soft and clear, and the bottom of the pan is slightly brown, but take care not to burn.

Meanwhile, soften the mushrooms in the reserved oil in a separate frying pan, then set aside.

Add the chicken giblets and salami (if using) and cook until brown. Add the steak, cook until brown. Stir in the tomato paste, tomatoes, spices and mushrooms.

Add just enough boiling water to cover the mixture (about 2 cups/500 ml), then partially cover the frying pan. Cook on low heat for 30 minutes, stirring occasionally, until nearly all the water is evaporated.

Serve over spaghetti cooked al dente, with a good sprinkling of freshly grated Parmesan cheese.

SERVES 4

# Roast lamb shanks

Perth is lamb-shanks party time! A feast, the likes of which I have never seen before in a cricket ground dressing room. At the WACA there is a bloke called Go Go, employed to handle catering at the famous cricket ground. He is of Indian origin and runs a restaurant in Perth.

Besides the normal food offered at dinner breaks during cricket matches, Go Go does something absolutely amazing with lamb shanks. They are so delicious, I blame them for distracting me during a one-day match against India when I was dismissed for a duck!

Prime time 'feeding hour on the shanks' is typically after matches. If you want to perform at your best, you are not going to chow down on a massive lamb shank before or during a match. So no one really has the desire to stuff their faces before warm up, or during the innings, with lamb shanks. But at the end of the game, we are that hungry, and Go Go brings them in and there is a roar of approval from the boys. We are like a pack of sharks going through bait fish! Bits and pieces are flying everywhere! The shanks have been sitting there all day marinating in their own juice. These special shanks are so tender that you have to cup your hands under them in case meat falls from the bone – and you certainly don't want to miss out on eating all of the delicacy.

People can go nuts over all types of things – cars, boats and diamonds. We go mad over Go Go's delicious lamb shanks!

I said to Go Go one day: 'Go Go, before I hang up my bat and retire, I am not letting you go until you show me how you cook your lamb shanks.'

He gave me a book on Indian curries which he signed with the words 'God bless Go Go'. And he then taught me about dhal and the lamb shanks.

What I see in Go Go is one of the best gifts anyone can give me – the gift of sharing his knowledge. For me, he opened the door to an entirely new way of roasting food.

MEAT

# Roast lamb shanks

Serve the shanks with the vegetables and a pile of mashed potatoes to soak up some of the pan juices. Ask your butcher to french (trim) the shanks for you.

8 frenched lamb shanks
2 tablespoons grated fresh ginger
4 garlic cloves, crushed
1 teaspoon salt
1 large brown onion, chopped
1 large carrot, chopped
1 large celery stalk, chopped

Preheat the oven to 250°C. Arrange the chopped onion, carrot and celery into a baking dish to make a bed to roast the shanks on. Lay the shanks onto the vegetables and put into the oven for 5 minutes, to seal the meat. Take the tray from the oven and reduce the temperature to 180°C.

Combine the ginger, garlic and salt in a small bowl. Spread over the meat.

Pour 1 cup (250 ml) of water into the dish and cover tightly with a double thickness of foil. Bake for 2 hours, until the meat is very tender and falling off the bone.

SERVES 4

# Straddie pizza

When you walk down the street in a place like Old Delhi in India, it is like winding the clock back 100 years, or even more. Early in 2004 while on tour, I walked through the centre of town and looked around in the early evening. I saw no cars, just pushbikes and ponies. And there on the footpath outside his shop was a shopkeeper with a single naked flame as his only light. He was selling fruit and vegetables. When was the last time you saw anyone in Australia living by candlelight?

How to maintain food with a chronic lack of electricity – leading to a lack of refrigeration – has always intrigued me. In the olden days in Australia, food was salted or smoked to preserve it. Well, those days still exist on the subcontinent.

In terms of flavour, nothing has changed in centuries. The same spices that were traded in very early times are still being used. The supreme taste of cold smoked meat or fish drives my desire to set up my own smokehouse. When I travel to cities around the world and I taste food that has been preserved without refrigeration, it is a constant reminder that one day I want a cold-smoker.

Straddie does have its own smokehouse, an old-style smokehouse at the local butcher's. There you can buy smoked legs of ham that are just divine on a pizza! Prosciutto is excellent on pizza, as well. And how I love eating prosciutto! It is a tasty food I come across frequently in Europe. As Kell and I have become more widely travelled, prosciutto and olives are two things we love to eat, particularly in Europe. Pizza laden with prosciutto, ham, bacon and olives is perfect for my life at home as well, and particularly when I am training because it can be eaten on the run, hot or cold.

Then again, if I am having some down time between tours – which for me usually falls in the winter months – then it is perfect served warm and eaten with a nice beer watching the footy. Believe me, when you have lived with Jimmy Maher, my Queensland Bulls team-mate, for four years, and you don't know how to make a pizza, you are in trouble. You can throw ingredients on a pizza base, put that in an oven for 15 minutes and Bob's your uncle!

Plus it also has the advantage of being eaten with your hands. I have always had a theory that any meal you grasp with your fingers is a good meal.

## Tomato paste

⅓ cup (50 g) pine nuts
1 cup (150 g) drained sundried tomatoes
2 tablespoons oil from the tomatoes
2 garlic cloves, chopped

## Pizza dough

7 g sachet dry yeast
½ teaspoon sugar
1 cup (250 ml) lukewarm water
2½ cups (375 g) plain flour
½ teaspoon salt
2 tablespoons olive oil

200 g thin slices prosciutto, chopped
200 g sliced leg ham, chopped
1 red onion, halved and finely sliced
1 red capsicum, cut into thin strips
1 cup (150 g) pitted Kalamata olives
200 g goat's cheese, sliced
olive oil and balsamic vinegar, to serve

# Straddie pizza

If you have a breadmaker, you can use it to make the pizza dough, but it is pretty quick and easy to make by hand. Check the manufacturer's instruction book for information if you want to use a breadmaker.

To make the tomato paste, put the pine nuts into a dry frying pan and cook over medium heat for about 3 minutes, until golden. Stir occasionally and be careful not to burn them. Put the sundried tomatoes, oil, garlic and pine nuts into a food processor and process to a rough paste.

Preheat the oven to 220°C.

To make the pizza dough, combine the yeast, sugar and water in a small bowl, and leave to stand for about 10 minutes, until the mixture is bubbly on top.

Sift the flour and salt into a large bowl and make a well in the centre. Pour in the yeast mixture and the oil, and mix with a wooden spoon, and then your hands, to a soft dough.

Turn out onto a lightly floured surface and knead the dough for about 5 minutes, until smooth (put more flour on the work surface as needed). Divide the dough into two portions, and roll each one out to about 30 cm round, to fit a lightly greased pizza tray. Bake for 5 minutes, until just half cooked.

Remove from the oven and, using the back of a spoon, spread tomato paste onto the pizza bases. Arrange prosciutto, ham, onion, capsicum, olives and goat's cheese on top. Bake for 15 minutes, until the base is crisp.

Drizzle extra virgin olive oil and balsamic vinegar over the pizzas just before serving.

SERVES 4–6

# Mango chutney

We were sitting in a fine Sri Lankan restaurant when I started talking to an elderly Sri Lankan woman who spends three weeks a year visiting her family in Melbourne. I have always loved Sri Lankan mango chutney and I ventured to ask this charming lady about it, and especially about the mangoes that go in it.

Much to my surprise, she told me how disappointed she always is with the standard of mangoes when she is in Australia – how they are far and away inferior to Sri Lankan mangoes. 'I can never get a decent mango in Australia,' she said.

'I don't wish to be disrespectful,' I replied, 'but our Bowen mangoes are bigger than a grapefruit and have more flavour than any mango in Sri Lanka!'

I told her a story about my brother, Gary, and I gorging ourselves on Bowen mangoes during the Christmas school holidays back on the farm near Kingaroy. We would eat so many mangoes, we got blisters around our mouths from the acid burning our skin. And because it was hot weather at Christmas time, we would often eat mangoes in our pool – the best place for eating mangoes, I can tell you! We didn't even have to get up and go to a tap to wash our faces and hands – we would just dunk ourselves under the water!

This almost-endless production line of mangoes came from one of my uncles, Tom. (Like another of my uncles, Pat, Tom was a Catholic priest who spent a lot of time in the communities of Bowen and the Diocese of Cairns. Both men have given years of service to the Catholic community in North Queensland.) If Tom didn't happen to visit over the Christmas period then, without fail, he would send down Bowen mangoes by the boxful. Gary and I would eat them until the cows came home! Tom's Bowen mangoes were – and still are – the finest mangoes I have ever tasted.

To prove my point, I cut a deal with the Sri Lankan lady: 'You show me how to make chutney and I'll send you down a case of Bowen mangoes when you're next in Melbourne.'

Thus, this traditional Sri Lankan chutney has made it into my kitchen.

SALADS, SIDES AND STUFF

# Mango chutney

*Be very careful when you are handling the hot chutney mixture, and keep the kids well away.*

2 kg ripe Bowen mangoes

3 teaspoons grated fresh ginger

2 cloves garlic, crushed

1½ teaspoons chilli powder

1 teaspoon mustard powder

½ cup (125 ml) vinegar

2½ cups (550 g) caster sugar

1 teaspoon salt

Peel the mangoes and cut the flesh away from the stone. Cut the cheeks in half lengthways, then into thin slices. Put the ginger, garlic, chilli and mustard powders into a small bowl and add 2 tablespoons of the vinegar. Stir to combine.

Put the remaining vinegar and the sugar into a large saucepan. Stir over low heat, without boiling, until the sugar has dissolved (this will take a while). Use a pastry brush dipped in water to clean sugar crystals from the side of the pan.

Add the mango and the spice mixture to the pan, and bring to the boil. Turn the heat down low, and simmer for about 1 hour, stirring occasionally, until the mixture is thick and pulpy. Stir in the salt.

While the chutney is cooking, thoroughly wash some glass jars and their lids. Put them in the oven (at about 150°C) to dry them thoroughly.

When the chutney is ready, ladle it carefully into the warm jars, and put the lids on tightly. Leave in a cool, dark place for about a month before using. The chutney will keep, unopened, for about 12 months. Once you have opened the jar, keep in the fridge for up to 1 month.

MAKES ABOUT 6 CUPS

# Dhal

In 1998, a year before my Test recall into the Australian team, I pleaded with the Australian chairman of selectors, Trevor Hohns, to select me in a group of fringe Test players embarking on a development tour of India. The small squad included several spin bowlers and two batsmen, Matthew Elliott and Greg Blewett, who were bound for Madras under the tuition of former Indian spin kings, Bedi and Venkat. I caught wind of the trip and begged Hohns to allow me to go. I said I would even pay my own way over. I told him I had a very strong feeling that I would be part of something special over there, and I just wanted a chance to experience the conditions.

But Hohns said the book was full, although if there was another chance in the future, I would be considered. Two days later the phone rang. 'I have some good news for you,' Hohns said. 'Greg Blewett has pulled out.' I couldn't pack my bag quickly enough!

We stayed at the ground in Madras, a venue where, three years later, I was to score a Test century. The interesting thing was that when I was with the development squad at the ground, I said to Matthew Elliott, 'I reckon I'll get a Test match hundred here one day.' It was like the throwaway line prior to my first ever Sheffield Shield match when I said my aim was to make the highest score by a Queenslander on debut, which I did. It is amazing! It is something I really believe, that as you think, so shall you become – that what you think about pretty much manifests itself in life.

While in India, Sri Lanka and Pakistan, a day does not pass without having dhal. Dhal forms part of the staple diet on the subcontinent. It is what you eat, whether you have a million dollars

or not a cracker. It is a very versatile meal. If you go to any restaurant or hotel, look at any menu or stop at any stall or market, you find dhal staring you in the face.

They cook it up in this big pot. Throw in coconuts, garlic, red chillies and water. Mix it up with tomatoes and that's it! They boil the hell out of it and away you go!

Even though I love seafood and meat, I also really enjoy the vegetarian food of the subcontinent. Dhal describes much about the subcontinent's culture. It is very deep and rich in colour, yet reasonably complicated because there is a lot you can do to it. Curl up your hands and use nature's tongs to eat it. It is either that or work for a year's salary to get some cutlery!

SALADS, SIDES AND STUFF

150 g (½ cup) yellow split mung beans (moong dal)

50 g (¼ cup) red lentils (masoor dal)

2 cups (500 ml) water

½ teaspoon turmeric

½ teaspoon salt

1 tablespoon olive oil

2 teaspoons cumin seeds

1 red onion, halved and finely sliced

4 garlic cloves, crushed

¼ teaspoon chilli powder

½ bunch fresh coriander, chopped

1 long green chilli, sliced

# Dhal

Dhal is delicious served as part of an Indian meal, with curries, rice and traditional accompaniments. It also makes a simple lunch, served with some warmed naan bread.

Put the mung beans and lentils into a sieve and wash under running water. Place into a saucepan with the water, turmeric and salt. Bring to the boil, then reduce the heat to low and simmer uncovered for about 20 minutes, until very soft and thick. Stir occasionally to prevent the mixture sticking to the bottom of the pan.

Meanwhile, heat the oil in a frying pan and add the cumin seeds. Cook over medium heat until just lightly browned. Add the onion and garlic and cook for about 10 minutes, until well browned. Stir in the chilli powder.

Add the onion mixture to the pan and stir to combine. Cook a further 3 minutes. Just before serving, stir in the fresh coriander and chilli.

— *You can use split red lentils, which are available from most supermarkets, but the split yellow mung beans are available from health food shops or specialty shops.*

SERVES 4

# Bruschetta

There is something simply delightful about Italy and the Italians' way of life. One time when I was playing county cricket in England, Kell and I had a week or so in Italy, where the weather was warm and the people flashy and enterprising. You expect Italian women to be dressed to the hilt, trying to catch a glimpse of themselves in shop windows; but it was the men who wanted to check out their reflections and see how snappy they were looking.

People-watching is a national pastime in Italy, made easy by the open piazzas and cobblestone streetscapes: you can spend dreamy hour after hour simply following your aroused senses, pricked by the aromas of freshly brewed espresso, tasting beautiful Italian ice-cream in freshly baked sugar cones. Italy is also appealing as I can move around inconspicuously, soaking up all the local specialties. From Rome to Pisa to Florence, over to the coast and then through Tuscany, where we sipped wines and soaked up the silence and the sun.

Italy is a magnificent tourist destination. For us it is the perfect place. I reckon both Kell and I should have married Italians because we love Italian food!

As a regular dish in the middle of the day when it was hot, we loved bruschetta with a Mediterranean salad. Italy has everything going for it: the people, the weather, the scenery, the history! But best of all, Italy is loved by us for its food – and its lifestyle surrounding food, where the after-lunch siesta halts your day and sends you into sleepy bliss.

SALADS, SIDES AND STUFF

# Bruschetta

This is a very versatile dish. You can try lots of different toppings, such as marinated capsicum, goat's cheese, feta, chopped olives - the list is endless. You can't really go wrong experimenting, so have fun!

4 Roma tomatoes, diced
1 red onion, finely chopped
1 sprig basil, finely shredded
2 garlic cloves, finely chopped
salt and pepper
1 loaf ciabatta or other crusty Italian-style bread
extra virgin olive oil and balsamic vinegar

Mix together the tomatoes, onion, basil, garlic, salt and pepper to taste in a bowl.

Cut 12 thick slices from the bread. Toast under a griller until golden brown. Cool, then top with the tomato mixture.

Drizzle lightly with olive oil and balsamic vinegar, and serve immediately.

SERVES 4

# Camembert dream pie

If you were wondering whether sports men and women of different sporting codes mix, the answer is yes. I once came across a wise old fella on my travels who said, 'Son, two of the most valuable assets in life are mentors and social wealth. For if ya got people to look up to, help ya learn a little quicker, and they just so happen to be people of good standing, take it from me, that's your edge.'

Personally I don't think it matters terribly much where you gather motivation, as long as every now and then you have a source. It's well known that I love rugby league and union, and I am a self-confessed surfing and fishing tragic. So when Andrew Ettinghausen ('ET') called and asked whether or not I would like to 'Escape with ET', I didn't even have to think about it. The next question was even better: 'How's South Africa sound?'

So off we went, flying first to Johannesburg for our connection to Durban, then driving for six hours to Sodwana Bay while taking in all the beautiful spots Qwa-Zulo Natal had to offer. There is nothing more exciting than a South African safari and this road trip was a cracker. It felt like the entire journey had taken no more than half an hour as we swapped every story our life experiences had given us.

Now it's important for readers to realise that ET, despite his heart-throb good looks, was one of rugby league's die-hard warriors — right up there as one of Australia's most capped players and the kind of player great enough to bridge generations due to his long-standing service to rugby league. A phenomenal player! An icon! I had so many expectations and so little time to find out about the man behind the man. It was time to get down to the business of trying to find a chink in this Titan's armour. ET's bravery was the test of the day and this game park was our venue. We arrived in the camp at night and it was pitch black.

'Haydos, I'll drop you off first and I'll take the car back to my camp,' ET stated. It was kick-off time.

Even though his tent was only a hundred metres away, the road back to his tent was convoluted, which would give me time to sneak up to his tent with darkness as my cover. Thinking he had deposited me safely in my tent, off he drove.

The plan worked. By the time ET arrived, I was crouching like a lion stalking its prey. The motor stopped and there was silence. Deadly silence! I could visualise ET, ears pricked for sounds, eyes sussing out any

possible moving form. Then, in the quiet heart of Africa, I could hear him coming towards the tent. Footsteps, moving closer, closer, closer. As his fingers fumbled for the zip, I leapt out from the back of his tent and ... sprung!

Never in my life have I heard such a blood-curdling, high-pitched screech: '*AAAAAAGH!*' Poor, old ET! This tough rugby league player was a blubbering mass of nerves, curled up outside his tent, paralysed with fear. Great bagging material!

'I thought you boys were fearless. Goes to show it's true, hey!', I said, sinking the teeth in a little further.

'What are ya talking about ya mongrel!', ET responded.

'The bigger they are, the harder they fall!' I said, stalking off as proud as punch.

Camping, safaris, animals, eskies, tents, tonnes of laughter and fun — all good things! A camembert dream pie, hot or cold, would have topped off this perfect safari.

spray olive oil

8 sheets filo pastry

1 teaspoon butter

2 onions, finely chopped

1 tablespoon brown sugar

1 tablespoon balsamic vinegar

5 rashers short cut bacon

3 eggs

¼ cup (60 ml) cream

salt and pepper

200 g round of Camembert, sliced

# Camembert dream pie

Preheat the oven to 180°C.

Spray a 23 cm pie dish or fluted flan tin lightly with oil. Spray the filo sheets lightly with oil, and stack together. Place into the dish and trim the edges.

Bake the pastry shell for 10 minutes, until golden brown. Set aside to cool.

Heat the butter in a frying pan and add the onions, brown sugar and balsamic vinegar. Cook over medium heat for about 15 minutes, stirring occasionally, until caramelised. Cool slightly. Spread the bacon, onions and camembert into the pastry shell.

Using a fork, whisk the eggs, cream, salt and pepper together with a fork. Pour over the filling and bake for about 20 minutes, until set and golden.

SERVES 6

# Cheese risotto

It's fair to say that while one of my first meals with Kell was a big hit, the venue definitely wasn't.

With my brother, Gary, his wife, Alex, and their two dogs, Kell and I went camping next to some obscure beach in northern New South Wales. Kell was taken by this meal I cooked – a chicken baked in the coals of a fire, after digging a hole in the sand and placing it into the ground. But she wasn't so sure about the camping!

I pulled up in my old army-green Kingswood with no tent – just a tarp, which I tied to the rear-view mirror and the limbs of a couple of trees. While Gary and Alex had a two-man tent, I don't think Kell was very impressed with her sleeping quarters!

She brought a doona with her and claims, 'Thank goodness I did. It was all I had to keep me warm – that and Gary's two dogs that snuggled up next to me!'

Though she had not known me for long, she was adamant about camping. 'No! No! No thanks – no camping!'

But she tried again. This time it was just Kell and I who ventured onto the northern NSW coastline. It rained solidly for four days!

'I didn't even get out of the tent for four days!' Kell tells people. 'When Matt was putting the tent up he cut off some lantana bush. While he was out surfing the ranger came around and gave me an earful for destroying the bush land! Having copped a tongue-lashing from the ranger, and enduring four days of rain, I packed the gear up while Matthew was out surfing and, when he returned, said it was time to leave. I have never been camping again!'

My cooking evolved from the bush camping days, and one of Kell's favourite meals now is a cheese risotto that I first whipped up for her one day in Melbourne while on tour in Australia.

SALADS, SIDES AND STUFF

1 tablespoon olive oil
1 large onion, finely chopped
2 garlic cloves, crushed
2 cups (440 g) arborio rice
1 cup (250 ml) white wine
3 cups (750 ml) chicken stock
¼ cup (25 g) grated Parmesan
50 g goat's cheese or goat's feta, chopped
½ cup (50 g) grated tasty cheese
salt and pepper
4 thin slices prosciutto, grilled until crisp

# Cheese risotto

This is a lazy risotto, rather than the traditional labour-intensive risotto which is continuously stirred. Sit down and relax with a glass of wine while it cooks!

Heat the oil in a large saucepan. Add the onion and garlic and cook until soft and lightly browned. Add the rice and cook, stirring, over medium heat for 3 minutes or until the rice turns clear.

Pour over the white wine and cook for about 5 minutes, until mostly absorbed. Add the stock, cover tightly and cook over low heat for 10–15 minutes, until the liquid is all absorbed.

Stir in the cheeses, put the lid back on and allow to stand for 2–3 minutes, until the cheese has melted. Season with salt and pepper to taste.

Serve the risotto straight away, with prosciutto crumbled over the top.

SERVES 4

# Cucumber salad

When I was a child up on the farm in Kingaroy, we used to follow intently the progress of my Uncle Pat's greyhounds.

The Gabba dogs used to be broadcast on radio but the only place we could get good radio reception was on the tractor. Dad would drive it up a hill, pull up the radio's aerial as high as he could, tune in and listen for Pat's most famous dog. We would all gather excitedly around the tractor.

We all celebrated when the dog won and he won often! In fact, he was the Australian record holder of 21 successive wins on his home track, Cairns, hence the reason for being celebrated as The King of the North. His real name was Stationmaster, so named because my mum's father was a stationmaster on the railways.

As my cricket career evolved, I would, of course, train at the Gabba where the dogs were run every Thursday evening. It was a tradition among the boys, headed by mad punter Trevor Barsby, to have a few drinks in the dressing rooms and watch the dogs race past us as they ran around the Gabba dog track, which used to be on the outside of the boundary fence.

In 1992, Pat was down from the north on holidays, and he knew a greyhound trainer called Maureen Culey and her husband, Bernie. He also knew they had a very pretty daughter and encouraged me to meet the family after training at the dogs. So I went to meet the Culeys with Pat, and that was the first time I laid eyes on Kell.

When I started going out with Kell, I had no idea at the time I would also be given a rail's run to a delightful side salad, a cucumber salad, cultivated by her greyhound-loving mother.

Whenever we have a barbecue with Kell's mum, cucumber salad is the go!

SALADS, SIDES AND STUFF

# Cucumber salad

This makes a great side salad at a BBQ.

2 telegraph cucumbers (or 4 Lebanese cucumbers)

salt

300 g carton sour cream

1 teaspoon grated fresh ginger

2 garlic cloves, crushed

2 tablespoons lemon juice

sweet paprika, to sprinkle

Peel the cucumbers and slice thinly. Place into a large bowl and sprinkle generously with salt. Cover and refrigerate for about 2 hours.

Squeeze with your hands to remove as much liquid as possible.

Mix the sour cream, ginger, garlic and lemon juice together, then stir through the cucumber. Put into a serving bowl and sprinkle lightly with paprika.

SERVES 6

# Avocado and mango salad

I am one of those lucky people who has the privilege of enjoying two Christmas gatherings each year with two different, very special families – with all my relations and with my cricketing family.

Every Christmas, due to the approaching Boxing Day Test match, Kell, Grace and our relations gather in Brisbane for a Christmas lunch several days before 25 December. It is a meal that everyone contributes to in some way and my Aunty Cay's contribution is to bring boxes of takeaway chicken and make her famous Avocado and mango salad. There is no better-tasting side dish than this wonderful mango salad, which is a showpiece that we like in the semi-tropics. It is hard to get a better mango or avocado than the ones offered in Queensland!

We eat till the cows come home and retreat to the pool.

Then I have my second Christmas with my cricketing family on Christmas Day. All the players' families come to Melbourne. There are mums and dads, children, wives and girlfriends.

You see your mates' lives unfolding as each year passes. You share a special time, a sacred time.

We congregate in the foyer of our hotel in the morning, then walk along the pathway by the side of the Yarra River en route to the Crown Casino where we are served an amazing meal. Father Christmas arrives and there is no question this bloke isn't Saint Nicholas. He is the real deal!

This is a prelude to the Boxing Day Test that, like the Melbourne Cup or a Bledisloe Cup Test, is a landmark day on the Australian sporting calendar.

For us, as cricketers, the week is a great celebration of what we do. You not only have Christmas but you have Boxing Day and the Test. It is a great week that I cherish.

SALADS, SIDES AND STUFF

the MATTHEW HAYDEN cookbook

128

3 rashers bacon

2 mignonette lettuces

2 mangoes, peeled and cubed

2 avocados, peeled and cubed

½ cup (65 g) unsalted roasted cashews, roughly chopped

Dressing

2 tablespoons extra virgin olive oil

2 tablespoons lemon juice

1 tablespoon French mustard

1 tablespoon thickened cream

# Avocado and mango salad

You could cook the bacon and prepare the lettuce and the dressing in advance, but don't put the salad together until it's almost time to serve.

Trim the bacon and cut into thin strips. Fry in a non-stick pan until brown and crisp, then drain on paper towels and leave to cool.

Pull the lettuce apart and wash and dry the leaves. Arrange the lettuce, mangoes and avocado in a serving dish. Sprinkle the cashews and bacon over the top.

Put all the dressing ingredients into a small screw-top jar, and shake like hell to combine.

Drizzle the dressing over the salad and serve immediately.

SERVES 10 AS A SIDE SALAD

# Vanilla slice

Travelling as a member of the Aussie Cricket team, I vividly recall sitting beside a curious American who worked for the Ford motor vehicle company in Detroit. We started swapping small talk and, suddenly, his curiosity got the best of him.

'What's with the uniform man? Ya in some sorta' team?'

'Yes, mate. I'm an Australian cricketer,' I answered proudly.

'Yeah?' he drawled. 'Now, there's one game I just don't get.'

At that moment I knew I was in for a long stay at the crease! Using baseball as an analogy, I explained, as simply as I could, the finer points of the game.

Periodically, he interjected. 'What? Get outta here! Ya mean ya play the game for five days and not get a result? What's the fun in that, man? Ya don't even get a winner or a loser! Damn! That's like kissing ya sister!'

My travelling companion was not to be deterred. I had the feeling this would be a long flight! A puzzled look, at times, appeared on his face but he pushed on. 'And what about those 4's and 6's?' he asked. I could see he was trying to put two and two together, but the concept of cricket just wasn't sinking in and the cultural barriers just weren't being bridged.

'So, yer actually telling me ya have 40 minutes for lunch and 20 minutes for tea breaks?'

I nodded, thinking I had appeased his curiosity. Not so! He was determined to learn as much as he could.

'So, man, I still just don't get it! Ya mean to say ya just sit in a room with nine men, a coach, and other staff for sometimes two whole days while the opposition is tryin' to bowl two men out?'

He struggled on, still trying to get the gist of the game.

'Whadda ya talkin' about? An' ya say the game hasn't changed in centuries?'

There was silence for a minute as he tried to take in some additional facts. Then he slowly leaned towards me and, weighing each word carefully with an added hand gesture as if trying to really make a huge effort to understand, he continued. 'Now, let me see if I've got this. Ya say the game can last for five days and ya can be in a room with most of ya team for sometimes two whole days, just sittin' around?' He stopped and shook his head. Then, sitting upright, he added quickly, 'Jeepers, man, whadda ya talk about in that time?'

I laughed and went on to tell him all manner of things are discussed. Of course, assessing the game is the most important, but many topics of conversation are put forward for non-serious discussion, too.

'Yeah! Like what?' he mused.

'Well, mate, topics like, who would make up The Most Talented Aussie Team, or The Ugliest Cricket Team in the World, or The Wankers Eleven ... All manner of things get ranked and talked about.'

He chuckled and added, 'You Aussies! Ya sure have a good sense of humour!'

Then, in a hushed tone, he continued, 'Do they feed ya, man?'

And so the conversation turned to food. I explained that the Australian team is very progressive in its approach to our diet, and that dietitians are employed to manage and give pertinent advice on the food we eat.

That exchange with my American companion led me to reflect on the food I've eaten at cricket grounds, from my early days at my beloved Brisbane Gabba, where I feasted regularly on a huge eye-fillet steak with chips; to my county cricket days in England where traditions were still followed by players like David Gower, who drank a cool Chardonnay with his lunch; and to Lord's, which boasts, rightfully so, of one of the best restaurants on the planet. 'Tea' was served in that wonderfully traditional English manner, with sandwiches, muffins, scones, jam rolls and other delicious sweet treats.

As Allan Border says when he wanders around the dressing room after 30 years of superb service to the game, 'Whatever happened to the good old days?' Being a lover of food, I must admit that I, too, miss those days when I could tuck into a wicked little treat!

The best treat I ever had was in 1997, when I was a pro for Hampshire County Cricket Club. They served these unbelievably delicious vanilla slices on trays at teatime. When it was cold and wet, the combination of the chilly English weather and the aroma of freshly made vanilla slices really tested my discipline. Let's see if they test yours as well!

As for my American friend and cricket ... well, I'm sure he still doesn't get it! He was a good bloke, though, and our chat did kill some time on the flight. Even better, we had a good old laugh.

# Vanilla slice

*So simple but tastes so ... good!*

2 sheets puff pastry

300 ml thickened cream

2 x 85 g packets instant vanilla pudding mix

2 cups (500 ml) milk

1½ cups (185 g) icing sugar

1 tablespoon soft butter

2 tablespoons boiling water

Preheat the oven to 180°C.

Put the pastry sheets onto two lightly greased baking trays and prick all over with a fork. Bake for 20 minutes, until they are puffed and golden brown. Remove from oven and set aside to cool.

Using electric beaters, whip the cream until soft peaks form. Put the vanilla pudding mix into another bowl and, using a wire whisk, stir in the milk.

Quickly fold the whipped cream into the pudding mix, then spread over the top side of one of the pastry sheets. Put the other sheet on top, flat side up.

Sift the icing sugar into a bowl and stir in the butter and water. Spread over the top of the slice. Leave for about 10 minutes, for the icing to set. Cut with a serrated knife into 12 pieces, and keep stored in the fridge.

MAKES 12

DESSERTS

# Coffee Cheesecake

There is nothing my mum and dad have not done for me, and their commitment to my life has been a major reason for my success.

There was a time when I was happy simply to follow in the footsteps of my father, grandfather and great-grandfather by farming our property at Kingaroy. As a youngster, I loved leaping into the tractor cabin, putting on ABC radio and working the land. Dad and I would cross each other in the field and give each other a wave as we went. I wanted nothing else in life!

Even today, when we go home to the farm, it gives me great pleasure to see my beautiful daughter, Gracie, riding on a tractor with Dad, and being showered with love by both Mum and Dad.

I can still hear Mum and Dad saying at different times, 'Matt, you can always come back to the farm if you really want to, but you must get an education first.' Both Gary and I knew we had to have a secondary education and then go on to university.

Mum and Dad encouraged me to follow Gary to boarding school at Marist Brothers College, Ashgrove, where my schooling and cricket benefited.

Distance was no barrier for my parents, even though at times they were hundreds and hundreds of kilometres away in Kingaroy. They have always been prepared to drop anything in support of their family. Dad bought his old Statesman from Sir Joh, or at least from the Premier's Department, and it has done the rounds!

As a young lad, when I was selected to play representative cricket, the kilometres that were covered were incredible. Sundays during the cricket season were spent travelling to Gympie, Bundaberg, Maryborough, the Sunshine Coast, Hervey Bay or Biggenden. An early start of around 5 a.m. was essential and often we would not get home until around 9 or 10 p.m. That was only at Wide Bay level – many more kilometres were added at Queensland level!

That old car carted me from one cricket match to another as a kid, and when I first started playing for

Australia, Mum, Dad and Gary jumped in the car and followed me around the country. To this day they think nothing of driving three hours if Kell needs a hand while I am away. They have been everything to me and the opportunities they have given me have made me the person I am today.

They have followed me to England when I played county cricket – though not in the Statesman! It was in England that Mum and Dad stumbled upon the finest dessert they have tasted – courtesy of Dad's cousin, Jim, and his wife, Helen.

The four were in England staying with us and Helen produced her classic dessert, coffee cheesecake, that was a huge hit. I am not a great sweets lover, but it was divine. It remains one of Mum and Dad's favourites, and with good reason.

DESSERTS

250 g packet milk arrowroot biscuits

3 teaspoons drinking chocolate

1 tablespoon instant coffee powder

125 g butter, melted

3 eggs, separated

3 tablespoons instant coffee powder

1 teaspoon vanilla essence

½ cup (125 ml) milk

1 tablespoon gelatine

¼ cup (60 ml) hot water

500 g cream cheese, at room temperature

1½ cups (330 g) caster sugar

300 ml whipped cream, to decorate

drinking chocolate, to dust

# Coffee cheesecake

Put the biscuits into a food processor and process until they form crumbs. Add the drinking chocolate and coffee powder and process briefly to combine. Add the melted butter and process until well combined. Spread out into a 24 cm springform pan, pressing firmly with the back of a spoon or the bottom of a glass to pack down the base. Put into the fridge while you make the filling.

Mix together the egg yolks, coffee powder, vanilla essence and milk. Put into a small saucepan and stir over a very low heat for about 5 minutes, to make a custard. Don't let this mixture boil. Transfer to a bowl to cool slightly.

Put the hot water in a small bowl and sprinkle the gelatine evenly over it. Leave for a few minutes to soften, then whisk with a fork to dissolve.

Put the cream cheese and ½ cup (110 g) of the sugar into a bowl and beat with electric beaters until smooth and creamy. Add the custard and the gelatine mixture, and beat to combine.

In another bowl, beat the egg whites until stiff, then gradually add the remaining caster sugar, beating constantly. Fold this into the cream cheese mixture and pour over the base. Put in the fridge to set for about 6 hours – but it is best made the day before.

Before serving, top with whipped cream and dust with drinking chocolate.

SERVES 10–12

# Mum's chocolate and macadamia nut pudding

My mum, Moya, really is a good cook even if she doesn't think so!

Dad's favourite dish, made by Mum, is Chocolate and macadamia nut pudding. It's one to die for!

As young kids, Gary and I used to sneak into the kitchen when Mum was cooking this dish, put our hands into the raw ingredients and pull out a fistful!

Today she tells us when we tease her unmercifully (but good-naturedly) about her cooking, 'Hang on! Wait a minute!' (We are always guaranteed to get a really good bite from Mum!) 'Where was my incentive?' she retorts. 'The raw ingredients were always gone – out the back door! Carried away on four healthy little legs before they even reached the oven! Anyhow … I have other talents!'

We have to agree with that. I'll even put it in writing.

Back to the dessert! It's really easy to make – hassle-free, simple and quick. (It has to be for Mum!)

The macadamia nuts are a must. The nuts come fresh from our Kingaroy farm. Out the back of the house we have a grove of macadamia trees and peach trees. The entire Kingaroy community is based around the nut trade. There would be about 20 or 30 macadamia nut trees that Dad planted when we were young fellas. These trees now produce more nuts than you can poke a stick at.

Dad collects the nuts and leaves them sitting on a piece of corrugated iron in a 'hold' shed. In summer, it gets so hot in that shed that the nuts almost roast. When it comes time to crack the nuts open, all these magpies that Dad has tamed gather around for the occasion.

I reckon Dad could tame a lion! He throws tiny pieces of nuts into the air and little willy wagtails swoop down and take the nut pieces before they can even reach the ground. Shouts of 'What a catch!' are often heard. Dad has all these magpies, too, eating out of the palm of

his hand. He gives them a couple of nuts and carries the rest of the nuts to Mum who serves them with the chocolate pudding and ice-cream. Delicious, especially in winter!

I have come to realise that, unlike me, Mum and Dad are sweet tooths!

Any kind of occasion – birthdays, Christmas – Mum is always encouraged by Dad to ensure we have his favourite dessert on the Kingaroy family farm menu.

DESSERTS

1 cup (150 g) self-raising flour
pinch of salt
2 tablespoons cocoa powder
¾ cup (160 g) raw sugar
½ cup (60 ml) milk
1 tablespoon melted butter
1 teaspoon vanilla essence
½ cup (70 g) chopped macadamia nuts
¾ cup (175 g) brown sugar
¼ cup (30 g) cocoa powder, extra
1¾ cups (435 ml) hot water
vanilla ice-cream, to serve

# Mum's chocolate and macadamia nut pudding

Try this with a shot of your favourite after-dinner liqueur.

Preheat the oven to 180°C.

Sift the flour, salt and cocoa powder into a bowl, and stir in the sugar. Add the milk, melted butter, vanilla essence and chopped nuts. Mix with a wooden spoon to smooth dough, and spoon into a 6-cup capacity deep ovenproof dish.

Mix the brown sugar and extra cocoa powder together and sprinkle over the cake mixture. Carefully pour the hot water in at the side. Bake for 45 minutes, then let stand for about 5 minutes.

Scoop out into bowls with plenty of the sauce, and a big scoop of vanilla ice-cream.

SERVES 4–6

# Honey-iced coffee cake

I have been extremely fortunate in my life, and I thank God every day for my many blessings. To wear the baggy green and be a part of such a great team – awesome! To travel the globe and play in venues all around the world – superb! To have the opportunity to experience other cultures and people from other countries – unbelievable! To make cricketing friends who remain great mates after cricket – the best! To get to know members of other cricketers' families – terrific!

It's well documented that I'm a big fan of Steve Waugh and his twin brother, Mark. They're both really good blokes, even though they come from 'Cockroach Country'! Although they're twins, they get ribbed by the rest of us for not spending much time together. My belief is they just have very different interests. But one thing they most definitely have in common is they both love to eat.

Mark eats like he's just heard the starting jingle at Harold Park race track and needs to place a bet on a hot tip. Steve reminds me of a jackal on the plains of Africa, eating on the run, pick-pocketing a skerrick here and a skerrick there from old man lion's kill. Considering there are four Waugh boys in the family, I reckon that dinnertime at the Waugh house would've been as competitive as their legendary backyard cricket games!

Mark has a very dry sense of humour, and he really likes to look good – hence his nickname, Pretty! A cracking bloke, he calls a spade a spade. I'll never forget being at a meeting one day when Mark spoke out. It was a serious discussion about tactics and play when suddenly, in exasperation, Mark said, 'Just hit the ball! You're talking about crap! It's rubbish!' Nothing breaks

up a group of fellas more than a statement like that,
I can tell you!

Steve is a real family man. He loves a good joke as
well as a good feed. We've often been partners in crime
when it comes to seeking a decent meal. There's an
unknown side, however, to this great Australian. His
collar doesn't always match his cuff!

Steve's a tremendous practical joker and loves
setting the stage for someone to make a fool of
themself. I'll always remember the morning after I'd
made 380 and Channel 9's Steve Leibmann interviewed
me. There I was, all set for a serious interview, but as
soon as the cameras were turned on me I was pelted
with mandarins, orange peel and apples. The moment
we all cracked was when one of those massive exercise
balls cannoned into the side of my head. Tracy
Grimshaw couldn't contain her laughter but poor old
Steve Liebmann was in a tight spot, trying to stay
professional. It was impossible to concentrate with Steve
whispering, 'Aren't you tired of talking about yourself
yet, Haydos?'

When I dobbed him in, I knew no one would
believe such an auspicious character as Steve Waugh
would be up to such mischief. Yet he was just showing
his true colours!

Steve truly has all the qualities most of us aspire to.
However, his athletic abilities are almost insignificant
when compared to his great sense of humanity, which
I believe is his number-one asset.

My mate has a sweet tooth, and I know he prefers
tea over coffee, but this next little sweet may change
that preference!

DESSERTS

3 teaspoons instant coffee powder

1 tablespoon hot water

125 g chopped butter, at room temperature

2 teaspoons vanilla essence

¾ cup (175 g) brown sugar

2 eggs

1 cup (150 g) self-raising flour

¼ cup (35 g) custard powder

⅓ cup (80 ml) milk

Honey Icing

30 g butter

1 teaspoon instant coffee

3 teaspoons hot water

1 teaspoon honey

1 teaspoon vanilla essence

1 cup (160 g) icing sugar, sifted

# Honey-iced coffee cake

If you can, use a shot of good espresso in place of the instant coffee. Serve with fresh flat whites and good friends.

Preheat the oven to 180°C. Grease a 20 cm ring tin with melted butter, and line the base with non-stick baking paper. Dissolve the coffee in the hot water and combine in a large bowl with the butter, vanilla essence, sugar and eggs. Sift the flour and custard powder into the bowl and add the milk.

Using electric beaters, beat on low speed until the ingredients are combined, then increase speed to medium. Beat for about 3 minutes, until very smooth and lighter in colour. Spoon into the prepared tin.

Bake for about 30 minutes, until a skewer comes out clean when inserted into the cake. Stand for 5 minutes before turning onto a rack to cool.

When cold, transfer to a serving plate and spread with the icing.

To make the honey icing, melt the butter, then stir in combined water and coffee, the honey, vanilla essence and half the icing sugar. Gradually stir in remaining icing sugar to mix a spreadable consistency.

SERVES 8–10

# Simple pavlova

England would have to be Ricky Ponting's and Damien Martyn's dream country! Picture this – a lush English golf course, an inviting little two-storey villa overlooking the 17th tee and an historic bridge over a lake that reflects an old English castle in the background. Golf fanatics, Punter Ponting and Marto would have thought they had died and gone to heaven if they had stumbled into the house Northamptonshire provided Kell and me with during an English county stint.

I hate built-up areas so when I signed to play county cricket as Northants captain, a priority was where I was going to live.

Northampton is really a spillway from London, only 90 minutes up the M1 from the English capital. Not being a suburban kid, I need space, trees and some lawn. I need the fresh air and this place was a sanctuary! It had a lake for fishing, country living, excellent outdoor areas, plus a gym and a pool.

It was as great a place as any to have mates over and former English batsman, Allan Lamb, was front and centre in that regard. He is such a character, a real man's man, and his wife, Lindsay, is a magnificent cook.

Because of the English summer twilight, often you don't get to sleep until 11.30 p.m., which gave Lamby and I time to train, then grab some irons and play a cheeky couple of holes in the fading light.

Lamby loves all the things that I love. He is a person who sees the lighter side of life and is one of cricket's great entertainers. Many a time he would put on a South African barbecue and we would bask in the afternoon sunlight with a special wine from his cellar.

Crawling before I walked in English cricket, I played league cricket first before entering the county scene.

After my first Sheffield Shield season, I played at Greenmount, alongside Toombull's Chris Holding. In the Greenmount side, too, were Gary and Phil Neville of Manchester United and English National team fame.

The Nevilles were a wonderful family. They were particularly good to Chris and me, taking us into their home for meals. The boys' dad was named Neville Neville, of all things. He was chairman of the Berry Football Club.

Gary was my opening partner, a real mongrel dog! A competitor! Phil was younger and had more cricket ability. He could have played for England as a cricketer, but at that time the pair's football careers were just starting off and the money coming in for a soccer career was amazing.

Meeting people like the Nevilles was a sign of the quality of people who were to come into my English life.

DESSERTS

# Simple pavlova

2 egg whites
1½ cups (330 g) caster sugar
1 teaspoon cornflour
1 teaspoon white vinegar
1 teaspoon vanilla essence
3 tablespoons boiling water
300 ml thickened cream
fresh fruit, for topping

Preheat the oven to 160°C. Line a baking tray with a sheet of non-stick baking paper.

Place the egg whites, sugar, cornflour, vinegar, vanilla essence and boiling water in a large bowl, and beat with electric beaters until stiff peaks form. At first the mixture will be very runny but persevere, it will take a good 5 minutes to get to the right consistency.

Pile onto the baking tray, and use a spatula or the back of a spoon to smooth out to about 22 cm in diameter. Bake for 20 minutes, until lightly brown. Remove from the oven and let cool on the tray. Slide a large knife under the pavlova and carefully manoeuvre it off the paper-lined tray onto a serving plate.

Whip the cream and spread over the pavlova, then top with fresh fruit.

SERVES 8

# Acknowledgments

My heartfelt thanks go to my incredible wife Kellie and beautiful daughter Grace. Their unconditional love and support has been such an amazing gift.

Mum and Dad, words seem superficial when it comes to describing the depth of your love and support. I only hope I can offer to my children the same elegant and gentle guidance you have given to me.

To Chris White, Angela Dawson, Lisa Stallard and all the staff at International Quarterback sports management company, my sincere thanks. With ten-and-a-half months out of every year a spent way from home, I know that the task of managing my life is far from easy. Your professionalism along with your innate ability to offer such personal service means the world to Kellie and me.

Andrew Dawson, you are an absolute champion of an individual. Thanks, mate, for the time and effort you have put into helping me with this project.

Thanks to Nanette Backhouse, Tracy Rutherford and the crew at ABC Books for their tireless efforts and patience with my first foray into book publishing. Their guidance has been invaluable.

Thanks also to the staff at James Street Markets and Zone Fresh for allowing me to use their markets for the photo shoots.

Cricket is truly a team game and I often wonder how different my life would be if I wasn't involved with such a talented and well-balanced group of individuals as these great Aussies, the 'Baggy Greens'. I would like to thank everyone in the Australian Cricket Team, but in particular Justin Langer and Steven Waugh. Friends for life, they've shared with me photographs, stories and opportunities, both on and off the hallowed turfs around the world. I'd also like to say thanks to Phil Hillyard, you are a great bloke to share a laugh and a beer with.

I know he'll perhaps be embarrassed by my thanks, but that's what makes this bloke so special. Guy Reynolds, thanks mate for your guidance and support. It seems like anything I can dream of you will back me one hundred per cent. You build people up, a rare and priceless gift. Cheers!

# Picture credits

Published by ABC Books for the
AUSTRALIAN BROADCASTING CORPORATION
GPO Box 9994 Sydney NSW 2001

Copyright © Matthew Hayden 2004

*First published November 2004*
*Reprinted February 2005*

ISBN 0 7333 1486 4

5 4 3 2

*Cover photographs: Vincent Long (front cover: top and bottom centre and*
   *back cover), Hamish Blair (front cover bottom left), Matthew Hayden*
   *(front cover bottom right).*
*Project management: Tracy Rutherford and saso content & design*
*Design: saso content & design*
*Food editor: Tracy Rutherford*
*Food photography: Andre Martin*
*Food stylist: Jane Collins*
*Lifestyle photography: Vincent Long*
*Additional photography see picture credits on page 159*
*Set in Stone Serif and Stone Sans by saso content & design*
*Colour reproduction by Colorwize Studio, Adelaide*
*Printed and bound by Tien Wah Press, Singapore*